I0009433

Samsung Galaxy Watch 7 Series User Guide for Beginners and Seniors

A Step-by-Step Manual for Mastering Your Smartwatch Features, with Large-Print Instructions for Easy Reading

Felix Klein Wagner

Copyright © 2025 by Felix Klein Wagner

All rights reserved.

No part of this book may be reproduced, distributed, or transmitted in any form or by any means, including photocopying, recording, or other electronic or mechanical methods, without the prior written permission of the author, except in the case of brief quotations used in reviews or critical articles and certain other non-commercial uses permitted by copyright law.

Samsung Galaxy Watch 7 Series
User Guide

for Beginners and Seniors

Felix Klein Wagner

Disclaimer

This user guide is intended for informational purposes only. While every effort has been made to ensure the accuracy, reliability, and completeness of the content, no guarantees are provided regarding its correctness or applicability.

The information in this guide is based on publicly available details about the Samsung Galaxy Watch 7 Series and Galaxy Watch Ultra. This manual is not affiliated with, endorsed by, or sponsored by Samsung Electronics Co., Ltd., its subsidiaries, or any related entities. All product names, trademarks, and brands mentioned are the property of their respective owners.

The author and publisher assume no responsibility for any issues, damages, or data loss resulting from the use or misuse of this information. Users are encouraged to refer to Samsung's official documentation, support channels, or authorized service providers for the most up-to-date and accurate information. Always follow Samsung's official guidelines and recommendations when using your Galaxy Watch 7 or Galaxy Watch Ultra.

Regarding Visuals

This guide provides detailed, step-by-step instructions in a written format, without relying on images, diagrams, or screenshots. This ensures that the information remains relevant and useful, even as Samsung updates its software, interface, or design elements.

For the latest visual references, users are encouraged to visit Samsung's official website or support pages. The absence of visuals keeps this manual lightweight, easy to navigate, and accessible to all readers.

With a focus on clarity and practical guidance, this guide is designed to help you understand, customize, and master your Galaxy Watch 7 Series or Galaxy Watch Ultra with confidence.

Why You Need This Guide as Your Ultimate Companion

Exploring a powerful smartwatch like the Samsung Galaxy Watch 7 Series can feel overwhelming—but not with this guide in your hands. Thoughtfully structured and written in clear, simple language, it walks you through every feature with ease. From setting up your watch and customizing the display to tracking workouts, monitoring your health, and using advanced tools like GPS, body composition, and sleep coaching—this guide covers it all.

Whether you own the Galaxy Watch 7 or the rugged Galaxy Watch Ultra, you'll find detailed instructions, smart tips, and real-world solutions tailored to your specific model. You'll also learn how to manage notifications, make calls, control music, use voice assistants, and extend battery life—all without digging through confusing menus.

More than just a manual, this is your everyday companion—designed to make sure you get the most out of your Galaxy Watch 7 Series from day one.

Table of Contents

Introduction

Welcome to Your Galaxy Watch 7 Series!

Congratulations on stepping into the world of smart living with the Samsung Galaxy Watch 7 Series. Whether you're here for better health tracking, seamless connectivity, or personalized style, you've chosen a smartwatch that offers cutting-edge technology wrapped in a sleek, wearable design. But this isn't just a watch—it's your fitness coach, health monitor, digital assistant, and lifestyle companion, all on your wrist.

This guide has been carefully created to help you get the most out of your Galaxy Watch 7 or Galaxy Watch Ultra. It's more than just instructions—it's a roadmap. You'll learn how to set up your device, personalize it to match your needs, explore its wide range of features, and use it effectively in your daily routine. Whether you're a tech enthusiast or a complete beginner, every section of this guide is written to be clear, supportive, and packed with practical insights to help you unlock the full power of your smartwatch.

The Galaxy Watch 7 Series isn't just about technology—it's about giving you real-time access to what matters. From your heart rate and sleep patterns to incoming calls, texts, and music controls, your watch keeps you informed and in control, without ever needing to reach for your phone. This guide will walk you through every function and feature so you feel confident, capable, and fully equipped from day one.

Meet the Family: Galaxy Watch 7 (40mm/44mm) and Galaxy Watch Ultra

The Galaxy Watch 7 Series offers options that suit different lifestyles and preferences. The Galaxy Watch 7 comes in two sizes—40mm and 44mm—both packed with essential smart features in a slim, lightweight frame. Designed for comfort and style, these models offer everything you need to stay connected, stay healthy, and stay on track. Whether you're monitoring your daily activity, checking your heart rate, replying to messages, or streaming music, the Watch 7 fits effortlessly into your routine.

For those who live more actively, push harder, or venture further, the Galaxy Watch Ultra brings a whole new level of performance. At 47mm, it's built for endurance and designed to go beyond the limits. With military-grade durability, enhanced water resistance, advanced GPS capabilities, and outdoor-focused features like a barometric altimeter and compass, it's the perfect match for athletes, explorers, and anyone who needs a watch that works as hard as they do. It also offers a larger battery, so you can rely on it for extended use in any environment.

No matter which model you've chosen, the Galaxy Watch 7 Series is packed with innovation and built to adapt to you. This guide will help you unlock every tool, feature, and shortcut—so you're not just wearing a watch, you're wearing a powerful extension of your lifestyle.

Quick Highlights: What's New and Why You'll Love It

The Galaxy Watch 7 Series brings meaningful upgrades that make everyday tasks smarter, faster, and more intuitive. At the heart of it is the new Exynos W1000 processor, designed to deliver smoother performance and faster response times than ever before. Whether you're switching between apps, starting a workout, or answering a call, everything feels fluid and effortless.

Health tracking has reached new heights with improved sensors for heart rate monitoring, blood oxygen levels, and body composition analysis. Sleep tracking now includes personalized coaching, giving you actionable insights instead of just raw data. The addition of irregular heart rhythm notifications adds an extra layer of wellness awareness that runs quietly in the background, helping you stay informed about your health.

If you're a fitness enthusiast, you'll appreciate the expanded workout library, auto-detection improvements, and enhanced GPS accuracy. The Watch Ultra adds adventure-ready features like a barometric altimeter, precision compass, and rugged durability that withstands more extreme conditions—ideal for hiking, mountain biking, or long-distance trail runs.

Battery life is another win. Optimized power-saving modes help your watch last longer when you need it most, and fast charging gets you back on track quickly. With LTE options available, you can even stay connected without your phone.

You'll also love the deep integration with your Samsung ecosystem. From controlling smart home devices to accessing your digital assistant or making payments on the go, the Galaxy Watch 7 Series does more with less effort—all from your wrist.

How to Use This Guide for Best Results

This guide is designed to be as easy to use as the watch itself. You don't need to read it cover to cover—unless you want to. Each chapter focuses on a specific area, so you can jump straight to the information you need. Setting up your watch? Head to Chapter 1. Want to improve your sleep quality? Flip to Chapter 4. Exploring outdoor features with the Ultra? Chapter 6 has you covered.

Every section is laid out clearly, using plain language and logical steps. You'll also find tips and recommendations sprinkled throughout—these are practical, real-world suggestions to help you get more out of your watch.

Use this guide as your personal reference. Bookmark key pages, highlight the features you use most, and don't be afraid to explore sections you haven't tried yet. The more familiar you become with what your Galaxy Watch 7 Series can do, the more powerful—and personal—it becomes.

Chapter 1

Getting Started

What's in the Box?

Opening your Samsung Galaxy Watch 7 Series box for the first time is an exciting moment. Whether you've chosen the sleek and compact Galaxy Watch 7 (available in 40mm or 44mm sizes) or the feature-rich and rugged Galaxy Watch Ultra (47mm), each model arrives thoughtfully packaged with everything you need to begin your smartwatch experience. Samsung's presentation is clean, organized, and user-friendly—designed to make setup simple, even for first-time smartwatch users.

Here's exactly what you'll find inside the box:

- **Galaxy Watch 7 or Galaxy Watch Ultra:** Your new smartwatch will arrive partially assembled, with one half of the strap already attached. Its screen and sensors are protected with a thin film you can peel off before use. The watch itself features a beautiful Super AMOLED display, a smooth casing, and precision-cut buttons.

- **Two Strap Sizes (S/M and M/L):** Samsung includes two strap sizes to ensure the best fit. These are soft, flexible silicone straps made for all-day comfort, whether you're heading to the office, the gym, or out on a weekend hike. Try both to see which provides the most secure yet comfortable fit. The bands are interchangeable with a simple click-and-swap design, allowing you to customize your style over time.

- **Wireless Magnetic Charging Cable (USB-C):** Your watch charges using a round magnetic puck that snaps onto the back of the watch. The USB-C connector plugs into any compatible wall adapter, power bank, or USB-C port. This charger supports fast charging, so you can get a day's worth of power in a short time.

- **Quick Start Guide and Documentation:** You'll find a printed foldout guide with basic instructions for powering on, pairing, and charging your watch. While this guide gives you a brief overview, the full user experience comes to life through the Galaxy Wearable app and this comprehensive user manual.

- **SIM Tray Tool (for LTE Models):** If you purchased an LTE model, the box may include a tiny pin tool used for eSIM activation or service carrier setup. Some models rely entirely on eSIM technology, so no physical SIM is inserted, but the tool may still be provided depending on regional packaging.

- **Safety and Warranty Leaflets (Region-Dependent):** Depending on your region, Samsung may include printed leaflets with product safety information, regulatory compliance notes, and warranty coverage details. These are useful to keep for future reference, especially if you ever need to contact support.

Before You Move On

Take a moment to lay everything out on a clean surface. Inspect your watch for any shipping damage (rare, but always worth checking), and ensure all listed items are included. Carefully remove any protective film or stickers from the watch face, sensors, and band.

Next, try on both straps to test which one suits your wrist best. A proper fit is important—not just for comfort, but also to ensure accurate readings for heart rate, sleep, and body composition measurements. The strap should sit snugly against your skin without pinching or leaving pressure marks.

Set aside the charging cable near a power source, and keep your smartphone close by with Bluetooth turned on. You're now ready to begin setup, and in the next section, we'll walk you through powering on your watch, pairing it with your phone, and taking your first steps with the Galaxy Watch 7 Series.

Your Watch at a Glance: Buttons, Display, and Sensors

Understanding the layout of buttons, display, and sensors ensures you'll feel confident navigating your device right from the start. Though sleek and minimal in design, your watch is packed with powerful tools beneath the surface—all strategically placed for ease of use, performance, and comfort.

Front: The Display

At the heart of your watch is a high-resolution Super AMOLED touchscreen display, available in two sizes for the Galaxy Watch 7 (1.3" on the 40mm model and 1.5" on the 44mm) and 1.5" on the Watch Ultra. The display is bright, colorful, and responsive, designed for clear visibility even in direct sunlight.

Depending on your model, you may also have a **digital rotating bezel** integrated around the edge of the screen. It lets you scroll smoothly through notifications, apps, and menus by turning your finger along the outer edge—no need to swipe.

On the right edge of the watch, you'll find two physical buttons that offer both functionality and quick access.

These buttons provide an alternative to touch gestures and are especially useful when your hands are wet, you're wearing gloves, or you're in motion during a workout.

Back: Sensors and Charging Surface

Flip the watch over and you'll find a polished sensor panel at the back of the case. This is where the magic of health tracking happens. The panel houses:

- **Optical Heart Rate Sensor:** Monitors your heart rate continuously or during workouts

- **Bioelectrical Impedance Sensor (BIA):** Measures body composition, including body fat percentage, skeletal muscle mass, and more

- **Electrical Heart Sensor (ECG):** Captures on-demand electrocardiogram readings (availability may vary by region)

- **SpO$_2$ Sensor:** Measures your blood oxygen levels throughout the day or during sleep

- **Temperature Sensor:** Monitors skin temperature, especially helpful for sleep insights and cycle tracking

The back panel also includes the **charging coil**, which connects magnetically to the included wireless charger. When placing your watch on the charger, make sure the sensors align with the puck to begin charging properly.

Other Built-In Sensors and Features

Though not visible, your Galaxy Watch 7 Series includes several internal components that enhance functionality, such as:

- **Accelerometer and Gyroscope:** For motion detection, workout tracking, and gesture controls
- **Barometer and Altimeter (Ultra only):** For elevation, air pressure, and weather-related data
- **Ambient Light Sensor:** Automatically adjusts screen brightness
- **Compass (Ultra only):** Supports outdoor navigation and direction finding
- **GPS + GLONASS + Galileo + BeiDou:** For precise location tracking during outdoor activities
- **Microphone and Speaker:** For taking calls, using voice assistants, and listening to media

Setting Up Your Watch for the First Time

Now that you're familiar with what's in the box and the physical layout of your Galaxy Watch 7 or Galaxy Watch Ultra, it's time to bring it to life. Setting up your watch for the first time is a simple, guided process that takes just a few minutes. Once complete, your watch will be fully connected, personalized, and ready to support your daily routine.

Step 1: Powering On Your Watch

Press and hold the **upper side button (Home/Power)** until the Samsung logo appears. This signals the watch is powering on. After a few seconds, you'll be greeted by the setup screen inviting you to connect your watch to a smartphone.

Step 2: Download the Galaxy Wearable App

To begin setup, you'll need the **Galaxy Wearable** app on your phone:

- For Android users: Open the **Google Play Store** or **Galaxy Store** and search for "Galaxy Wearable."

- For iPhone users: Open the **App Store** and download **Samsung Galaxy Watch (Gear S)**. Note that functionality may be limited on iOS.

Once downloaded, open the app and ensure **Bluetooth is turned on** on your phone.

Step 3: Start the Pairing Process

Tap **"Start"** in the Galaxy Wearable app. Your phone will search for available devices. When your watch appears in the list, tap to select it. A pairing code will be displayed on both devices—verify that the codes match and then confirm on both your phone and watch.

If your watch has LTE capability and you're activating cellular service, the app will prompt you to follow additional steps to connect with your carrier. This may include logging into your mobile provider account or scanning a QR code.

Step 4: Grant Permissions and Customize Settings

The app will ask you to grant various permissions for optimal functionality:

- **Access to contacts, messages, calendar, and call logs** so your watch can display and manage notifications
- **Location access** for accurate GPS tracking and weather updates
- **Notification permissions** so the watch can mirror alerts from your phone
- **Samsung Health access** to sync activity, sleep, heart rate, and body composition data

You'll also be prompted to **sign in to your Samsung account**, which is required to access cloud backups, the Galaxy Store, Samsung Health, and more. If you don't have one yet, you can create one during setup.

Step 5: Install Recommended Apps and Watch Faces

Once permissions are granted, you'll have the option to install recommended apps like Samsung Health, Samsung Pay, SmartThings, and additional watch faces. You can always skip this for now and return to it later via the Galaxy Wearable app.

Step 6: Update Software

Before completing setup, your watch may check for firmware updates. If an update is available, allow it to install. This ensures you have the latest features, performance enhancements, and security patches from day one.

Step 7: Customize Basic Settings

Next, you'll set a few basic preferences:

- Choose your preferred **watch face**
- Set display brightness and screen timeout
- Enable features like **raise to wake**, **Do Not Disturb**, and **gesture controls**
- Adjust haptic feedback and sound settings

Step 8: Explore Your Watch

Once setup is complete, your watch will display the main watch face, and you're ready to explore. Swipe left and right to browse widgets, swipe down for quick settings, and press the Home button to access your apps. The Galaxy Wearable app on your phone will remain your main control center for customizing the experience further.

Helpful Tips for Day One:

- Keep your watch snug but comfortable on your wrist for accurate sensor readings.
- Start with a basic watch face and explore more advanced options later.
- Charge your watch fully before your first full day of use.
- Explore the **Samsung Health** app to connect deeper wellness insights.

Connecting to Your Phone (Android or iOS)

Pairing your Galaxy Watch 7 or Galaxy Watch Ultra with your smartphone is what unlocks its full functionality—from receiving notifications to syncing health data and installing apps. Samsung makes the connection process seamless for Android users, and relatively smooth for iOS users, though with some feature limitations.

For Android Users (Best Compatibility):

1. **Ensure Bluetooth is enabled** on your Android smartphone.
2. **Download the Galaxy Wearable app** from the Google Play Store or Galaxy Store.

3. **Open the app**, tap "Start," and select your device from the list when it appears.

4. Confirm the **pairing code** on both your phone and watch.

5. Once paired, follow the guided steps to grant permissions, sign in to your Samsung account, and customize basic settings.

With Android, you'll enjoy full compatibility—including app notifications, call and message sync, Samsung Health integration, and access to the Galaxy Store for additional apps and watch faces.

For iPhone Users (Limited Compatibility):

1. **Turn on Bluetooth** and install the **Samsung Galaxy Watch (Gear S)** app from the App Store.

2. Open the app, tap "Start the Journey," and choose your Galaxy Watch model.

3. Select your watch when it appears, confirm the pairing code on both devices, and proceed with on-screen instructions.

iOS users can still receive notifications, track health data, and use core features, but some functions—like Samsung Pay, replying to messages, and third-party app syncing—may be limited.

Tip: For best performance and feature access, Samsung recommends pairing your Galaxy Watch with a Samsung Galaxy phone or Android device.

Getting Familiar with Navigating Menus and Screens

Your Galaxy Watch is designed to be intuitive, responsive, and easy to use—whether you're swiping through widgets, opening apps, or customizing your settings. Here's how to move around with confidence:

Basic Gestures

- **Swipe Left:** Access widgets like steps, heart rate, weather, calendar, and more.

- **Swipe Right:** View your notifications. Tap on any notification to read more, dismiss, or interact with it.

- **Swipe Up:** Open the full app menu. You'll see icons arranged in a circular or grid layout.

- **Swipe Down:** Access Quick Settings (Wi-Fi, Airplane mode, Sound, Battery saver, etc.).

Quick Settings Panel (Swipe Down)

Here, you'll find commonly used settings like:

- Brightness
- Battery percentage
- Do Not Disturb
- Wi-Fi toggle
- Theater mode
- Flashlight
- Sound/vibration toggle

Customizing Your Menu Layout

You can rearrange apps and widgets to place your most-used features front and center. This can be done directly on the watch or through the Galaxy Wearable app on your phone.

Tip: If you ever feel lost, press the upper button to return to the home screen.

Once you've spent a few minutes swiping around and tapping through the menus, the navigation will feel natural.

Touchscreen and Button Basics You Should Know

Mastering the touchscreen and buttons on your Galaxy Watch 7 or Galaxy Watch Ultra will make navigating your device smooth, fast, and intuitive. Whether you're browsing apps, checking notifications, or adjusting settings, understanding these basic controls helps you use your watch more efficiently—right from the start.

Touchscreen Basics

The Galaxy Watch 7 Series features a responsive Super AMOLED display that supports multi-touch gestures. Here are the essential touchscreen actions:

- **Tap:** Select apps, open features, confirm selections, or activate on-screen buttons.

- **Swipe Left or Right:** Move between widgets or screens. Left swipes typically reveal your widgets (steps, heart rate, weather), while right swipes access your notifications.

- **Swipe Up:** Open the app drawer to access all installed apps.

- **Swipe Down:** Access the quick settings panel (brightness, sound, airplane mode, battery saver, etc.).

- **Touch and Hold:** Long press the watch face to enter customization mode, or on an app to move or uninstall it.

- **Raise-to-Wake:** Lifting your wrist will automatically wake the screen if enabled in settings.

- **Double Tap Screen (if enabled):** Wake the screen without pressing a button.

Tip: You can adjust touch sensitivity in the settings, which is helpful if you wear gloves or need more responsive control.

Button Basics

Your watch features two side buttons on the right edge:

1. **Top Button – Home/Power/Bixby**
   - **Single Press:** Return to the watch face or open the app screen.

   - **Double Press:** Launch a shortcut (customizable in the settings; often defaulted to recent apps or workouts).

   - **Press and Hold:** Launch Bixby or bring up the power menu (restart, power off).

   - **When Screen is Off:** Press once to wake the screen.

2. **Bottom Button – Back/Function**

○ **Single Press:** Go back to the previous screen or menu.

○ **Press and Hold:** Can be customized—by default, it may trigger the emergency SOS feature if held for a few seconds.

Using Both Buttons Together

- **Take a Screenshot:** Press the top and bottom buttons **simultaneously**. Screenshots are saved in the Gallery and can be viewed on your phone.

Digital Rotating Bezel (If Equipped)

If your model includes the digital bezel feature:

- Slide your finger along the edge of the display in a circular motion to scroll through apps, notifications, or settings. It mimics the physical rotating bezel found on older models and offers quick, tactile navigation.

Customizing Button Functions

You can personalize what double presses or long presses do by going to:

Settings > Advanced Features > Customize Keys. This allows you to assign your most-used feature—like workouts, voice assistant, or your favorite app—to a button shortcut.

Chapter 2

Personalizing Your Galaxy Watch

Choosing Your Favorite Watch Face

One of the most exciting parts of owning a Galaxy Watch 7 or Galaxy Watch Ultra is making it reflect your personal style. Your watch face isn't just for telling time—it's a blend of aesthetics and function that sets the tone for your entire experience. Whether you prefer a minimalist digital look, a traditional analog style, or a data-rich fitness dashboard, there's a perfect watch face waiting for you.

Browsing Built-in Watch Faces

Samsung includes a diverse collection of built-in watch faces designed to suit every taste and purpose. To explore and change them directly on your watch:

1. **Touch and hold the current watch face** on your screen until it shrinks and a selection menu appears.

2. **Swipe left or right** to browse available faces. You'll find analog faces, digital clocks, health-focused dashboards, minimalist options, animated designs, and more.

3. Tap the one you like to apply it instantly.

You can also **customize each face** by tapping the **"Customize"** button beneath the preview. This allows you to adjust:

- **Color schemes**

- **Font styles**

- **Background patterns**

- **Information "complications"** (such as steps, battery life, heart rate, weather, calendar events)

Downloading More Watch Faces

If you want even more options, head to the Galaxy Wearable app on your phone:

1. Open the **Galaxy Wearable** app.
2. Tap **"Watch Faces."**
3. Browse featured faces or tap **"Discover More"** to open the **Galaxy Store.**
4. Search by category, popularity, or developer.
5. Download both free and premium watch faces to expand your collection.

Once installed, the new faces will appear in your watch's face selection screen.

Using Third-Party Watch Face Apps

If you're looking for something completely unique, apps like **Facer** and **WatchMaker** provide thousands of customizable options. These apps allow you to create your own face or choose from user-created designs, often themed around art, productivity, or pop culture.

To use a third-party app:

1. Download **Facer** or **WatchMaker** from the Galaxy Store or Google Play.
2. Browse and install watch faces via the app.
3. Select the synced face on your watch or through the Galaxy Wearable app.

Setting Up an Always-On Display (Optional)

Want to keep your watch face visible at all times? Enable the Always-On Display:

1. Go to **Settings** > **Display** > **Always On Display.**
2. Toggle it on to show a dimmed version of your watch face when the screen is idle.

Keep in mind this feature may reduce battery life, but it provides a traditional timepiece look.

Creating a Signature Look

Don't be afraid to change your watch face depending on your mood, activity, or outfit. Use a professional analog look for meetings, a sporty dashboard for workouts, or a vibrant animated face for casual days.

Customizing the Look (Colors, Styles, and Themes)

Samsung understands that every user has unique preferences, which is why the Galaxy Watch 7 Series and Galaxy Watch Ultra offer extensive customization options. You can personalize every visual aspect of your watch, from vibrant colors and stylish watch faces to minimalistic themes and intuitive layouts. Whether you prefer a bold, eye-catching display or a simple, elegant interface, you can tailor your watch to match your style and needs.

Watch Face Customization: Colors, Fonts, and Layouts

Start with your watch face—the most visible and frequently interacted part of your device. Every watch face comes with a variety of styling options that let you:

- **Choose color themes** for the background, hands (in analog styles), numerals, and accent lines

- **Adjust the font type and thickness** to reflect your style—sleek and modern, bold and sporty, or elegant and classic
- **Select layout configurations** for the clock, date, and complications (mini-data panels)
- **Swap digital vs. analog styles,** or choose hybrid options for the best of both worlds

To access these settings directly from your watch:

1. **Touch and hold** the watch face until the selection carousel appears
2. Swipe to find the face you want and tap **"Customize"**
3. Use the swipe gesture to move between customization pages—each one will let you edit a specific part like color, style, or data fields
4. Tap each editable area and scroll through the available options
5. Tap **OK** or the checkmark to save your changes

Advanced Customization via Galaxy Wearable App

The Galaxy Wearable app offers a more detailed view and easier controls when fine-tuning your watch's appearance.

1. Open the **Galaxy Wearable app** on your phone
2. Tap **"Watch Faces"** and select the current face or browse new ones
3. Tap **"Customize"** to open the editing menu
4. You'll be able to preview changes in real time on your phone screen before applying them to the watch
5. Tap **"Apply"** when you're satisfied with the look

This app-based method is especially helpful when editing intricate faces with multiple complication fields or color zones.

Complications: Small Widgets with Big Value

A key part of visual customization lies in **complications**—those tiny, interactive data widgets embedded into your watch face. You can choose to display:

- Step count
- Heart rate
- Battery percentage
- Weather info
- Calendar events
- Sunrise/sunset times
- Workout shortcuts
- App launch icons (like Messages, Samsung Health, or Music)

You can mix and match these complications depending on how you want to interact with your watch. Some watch faces support up to 4 or 5 complication slots, while others are more minimal with 1 or 2. You can also remove all complications if you prefer a clean, time-only design.

Using Themes and Background Effects

For supported watch faces, you can also customize the **background pattern**, **texture**, or even **add animated effects** like moving weather icons or interactive fitness rings. These small touches bring your watch to life in a dynamic, fun way.

Personalizing Your Home Screen

Your home screen is where functionality meets convenience. Customizing it properly means you can access what you need quickly—without digging through apps or menus. Whether you want instant access to your step count, calendar events, or favorite workouts, the Galaxy Watch gives you complete control over how your information is displayed.

Customizing Tiles (Widgets)

Tiles are the swipeable cards that appear to the left of your main watch face. Each one represents a different tool or app. You can think of them like "glanceable apps" that show live, useful data.

*To customize tiles on your **watch**:*

1. Swipe left from your watch face to scroll through current tiles
2. When you reach the end, tap the "+" (**Add Tile**) button
3. Select from a list of available tiles like Heart Rate, Weather, Sleep, Calendar, Alarm, Music, and more
4. To **rearrange**, touch and hold any tile, then drag it to a new position
5. To **remove**, swipe to the tile you want gone, touch and hold, then tap the red minus (–) icon

*To customize tiles using your **Galaxy Wearable app**:*

1. Open the app and tap **"Tiles"**
2. You'll see a complete list of active and available tiles
3. Drag and drop to reorder, or tap **"Add"** to include new ones
4. Tap the red circle to remove unwanted tiles

Customizing App Layout

Your Galaxy Watch apps appear in either a **grid view** (default) or a **list view**, depending on your settings. You can change this layout and reorder apps for easier access.

To change app layout:

1. Go to **Settings > Apps > App View**
2. Choose **Grid View** (with circular icons) or **List View** (with names beside each app)

To reorder apps:

1. On the watch, press the **Home button** to open the app screen
2. Touch and hold any app icon until you can drag it
3. Move the icon to the desired position and release

You can also customize the app layout via the **Galaxy Wearable app** under **Apps > Reorder**.

System Appearance and Accessibility Enhancements

You can further fine-tune your home screen's visibility and performance under **Settings > Display**:

- **Adjust brightness manually** or set it to auto
- **Set screen timeout** for how long the display stays on after interaction
- **Enable Touch Sensitivity** if using gloves
- **Switch to dark mode** for better night-time visibility
- **Activate larger fonts or high-contrast mode** for easier readability

For users who need additional accessibility options, features like **screen readers, color inversion, grayscale modes**, and **gesture assistance** are available under **Settings > Accessibility**.

Adjusting Display Settings for Comfort and Convenience

Brightness Settings

To ensure visibility in all lighting conditions:

1. Go to **Settings > Display > Brightness**
2. Use the slider to adjust brightness manually, or toggle on **Auto Brightness** to let the watch adapt to your environment

Auto Brightness is perfect for day-to-night transitions, but if you prefer control, manual brightness ensures a consistent display level throughout the day.

Screen Timeout

This controls how long the screen stays active after you interact with it. A shorter timeout saves battery, while a longer one gives you more time to read data.

1. Navigate to **Settings > Display > Screen Timeout**
2. Choose from several options (15 seconds to 5 minutes) based on your needs

Tip: For workouts or tasks where you're checking stats often, increasing the timeout prevents constant reactivation.

Touch Sensitivity

If you wear gloves or need more responsive input, enable high-touch sensitivity:

1. Go to **Settings > Advanced Features > Touch Sensitivity**
2. Toggle it on for better screen response through fabrics

Font and Text Size

Customize font size and style for easier readability:

1. Go to **Settings > Display > Font Style and Font Size**
2. Select your preferred typeface and adjust the text size with the slider

Raise to Wake and Tap to Wake

These features turn on the screen without pressing buttons:

- **Raise to Wake:** Activates the screen when you lift your wrist
- **Touch to Wake:** Double tap the screen to activate

  To enable/disable these, go to **Settings > Display > Wake-up gestures**

Night Mode and Theater Mode

For darker environments, these modes reduce light disturbance:

- **Night Mode:** Found under **Settings > Display**, dims colors and reduces screen brightness
- **Theater Mode:** Temporarily disables wake gestures and alerts. Enable from **Quick Settings** panel (swipe down on the watch face)

All of these display options ensure your Galaxy Watch fits comfortably into your daily flow, whether you're under the sun, in the office, or winding down at night.

Personalization Tips

- **Match your watch face to your outfit or activity.** Use sleek analog faces for business settings, digital dashboards for workouts, and playful animated styles for casual days.

- **Use complications wisely.** Add health stats during workouts, battery level for busy days, or calendar reminders for productivity

- **Rotate through different looks.** Long-press to swap watch faces quickly when transitioning from work to gym to dinner

- **Keep it battery-friendly.** Avoid heavy animations or multiple live complications if battery life is a concern

- **Clean up unused faces.** In the Galaxy Wearable app, long press any saved face and remove it to declutter your library

Chapter 3

Staying Connected

Managing Bluetooth and Wi-Fi Connections

Bluetooth: Your Primary Connection to Your Phone

Bluetooth is the main way your watch communicates with your smartphone. It handles everything from syncing notifications and health data to allowing phone calls, message replies, and app management.

To Pair Your Watch with a Phone (If Not Already Paired):

1. Open the **Galaxy Wearable** app on your smartphone.
2. Ensure **Bluetooth is enabled** on your phone.
3. Follow the prompts to **search for available devices** and connect.
4. Confirm the **pairing code** on both the watch and the phone to establish the connection.

Once paired, your watch will automatically reconnect to your phone whenever Bluetooth is active and in range.

Check Bluetooth Status on the Watch:

1. Swipe down from the watch face to open **Quick Settings**.
2. Look for the **Bluetooth icon** (shaped like a 'B' with triangular spikes).
3. If it's grayed out, tap to enable it.

To Manually Enable or Disable Bluetooth:

- Go to **Settings > Connections > Bluetooth**
- Toggle the switch on or off as needed
- You can also pair Bluetooth headphones or earbuds from this menu for listening to music directly from your watch

When to Use Bluetooth:

- When your phone is nearby
- For real-time syncing of health data and app notifications
- For calling or messaging from the watch (non-LTE models require Bluetooth for this)

Wi-Fi: Keeping You Connected When Bluetooth Is Out of Range

Wi-Fi on your Galaxy Watch acts as a secondary connection method when Bluetooth isn't available. If your phone is out of range but connected to the internet, your watch can still receive notifications, access apps, and even sync data—provided it's connected to a Wi-Fi network.

How to Connect to Wi-Fi:

1. On your watch, go to **Settings > Connections > Wi-Fi**
2. Tap **Wi-Fi** to turn it on
3. Select **"Wi-Fi networks"** to scan for available connections
4. Tap the network name and enter the password using the on-screen keyboard
5. Tap **Connect**

Tip: If your phone is connected to the same network and paired via the Galaxy Wearable app, your watch can automatically inherit saved Wi-Fi credentials without manually entering passwords.

Wi-Fi Modes:

- **Auto:** Automatically turns on Wi-Fi when Bluetooth is disconnected
- **Always On:** Keeps Wi-Fi active even if Bluetooth is connected
- **Off:** Disables Wi-Fi completely (saves battery)

To choose your mode, go to **Settings > Connections > Wi-Fi > Wi-Fi Settings > Wi-Fi Networks > Advanced** and select your preference.

When to Use Wi-Fi:

- When you're at home, work, or a public location with a trusted network
- When your phone is not nearby but connected to the internet
- When downloading large apps, software updates, or syncing media

Switching Between Connections Seamlessly

Your Galaxy Watch is smart enough to switch between Bluetooth and Wi-Fi automatically to keep you connected. For example, if you walk away from your phone, the watch will drop the Bluetooth connection and, if available, switch to Wi-Fi without any input from you.

Pro Tip:

For uninterrupted communication when you're truly away from your phone, consider an LTE model of the Galaxy Watch 7 Series. With LTE activated through your carrier, your watch can stay connected to calls, texts, and apps completely independent of your phone.

LTE Connectivity Explained (for LTE Models)

If you own the LTE version of the Galaxy Watch 7 or Galaxy Watch Ultra, you've got a powerful advantage: the ability to stay connected without your phone. LTE gives your watch independent access to calls, messages, apps, streaming, and location services—even when your phone is turned off or far away.

What is LTE on a Smartwatch?

LTE (Long-Term Evolution) is the same mobile network technology used by your smartphone. When activated through a carrier, your Galaxy Watch LTE can connect directly to mobile networks, enabling it to function like a mini-phone on your wrist.

What You Can Do with LTE:

- Make and receive phone calls
- Send and receive text messages
- Stream music and podcasts
- Use GPS and maps for navigation
- Access apps and data services
- Get notifications and sync with Samsung Cloud
- Use Samsung Pay (if supported by region and carrier)

How to Set Up LTE on Your Watch:

1. **Contact Your Carrier**
   - LTE functionality requires a compatible data plan. Reach out to your mobile provider and ask about smartwatch plans.

- Some carriers offer Number Sharing (your watch shares your phone number), while others assign a separate line.

2. **Use the Galaxy Wearable App**
   - Open the **Galaxy Wearable** app on your phone
   - Tap **Mobile Plans > Add Mobile Plan**
   - Follow the prompts to connect to your carrier's setup portal
   - Confirm plan activation and complete verification steps

3. **eSIM Activation**
   - The Galaxy Watch 7 Series uses an **embedded SIM (eSIM)**, so there's no need to insert a physical SIM card
   - Setup is entirely digital and takes only a few minutes with the correct carrier support

How to Manage LTE Settings on the Watch:

- Go to **Settings > Connections > Mobile Networks**
- Toggle LTE on or off
- Choose when to use LTE:

   - **Auto**: LTE turns on only when Bluetooth and Wi-Fi are unavailable
   - **Always On**: LTE stays active at all times (uses more battery)
   - **Off**: Disables LTE manually

Battery Tip: LTE consumes more power, especially during voice calls or heavy streaming. To maximize battery life, use LTE only when needed or keep it on Auto mode.

Receiving and Responding to Notifications Easily

Your Galaxy Watch 7 Series is designed to keep you informed without interrupting your flow. Once connected, your watch mirrors key notifications from your phone—allowing you to stay on top of messages, calls, app alerts, calendar events, and more, directly from your wrist.

How Notifications Work:

- When paired via Bluetooth or Wi-Fi (or LTE), your watch displays alerts from your phone in real time
- You can view, dismiss, or interact with them depending on the app and your preferences
- Notification vibrations or sound can be customized based on your activity or focus

Enabling Notifications:

1. Open the **Galaxy Wearable** app on your phone
2. Tap **Watch Settings > Notifications**
3. Toggle on **"Show phone notifications on watch"**
4. Select **"Show alerts even when phone in use"** if you want to see notifications even when actively using your phone
5. Scroll down and enable or disable notifications from specific apps—this helps reduce clutter and prioritize what matters

Viewing Notifications on the Watch:

- Swipe **right** from the main watch face to access the notification panel
- Tap any alert to expand and read more

- Use the digital bezel (if available) or swipe vertically to scroll through longer messages
- Tap the **dismiss icon (X)** to remove the notification
- Long-press a notification to access settings or block future alerts from that app

Replying to Messages and Emails:

- Tap the notification
- Choose a reply method:
  - **Voice dictation**
  - **Keyboard**
  - **Pre-set Quick Replies** (e.g., "I'll call you back," "OK," "Sounds good")
  - **Emoji response**

- Tap **Send** to deliver your response directly from the watch

You can **customize your Quick Replies** in the Galaxy Wearable app:
 Watch Settings > Notifications > Quick Responses

Managing Notification Style and Behavior:

- Go to **Settings > Notifications** on your watch
- Adjust sound, vibration, or mute alerts
- Enable **Smart Relay**, which shows full notification content on your phone when you pick it up
- Use **Do Not Disturb**, **Theater Mode**, or **Bedtime Mode** to silence notifications temporarily

Pro Tips for Notification Management:

- Use app filters to receive only the most important alerts
- Turn off social media or promotional app notifications to reduce distraction
- Enable message previews if you want to read full texts from the notification bar
- Use vibration-only alerts during workouts or meetings

Making and Answering Calls from Your Wrist

One of the standout features of the Galaxy Watch 7 and Galaxy Watch Ultra is the ability to handle phone calls right from your wrist. This functionality allows you to stay connected without reaching for your phone—ideal for moments when you're in a meeting, cooking, exercising, or on the move. Whether you're using a Bluetooth-only model or an LTE-enabled one, your Galaxy Watch is fully equipped to keep the conversation going.

Bluetooth vs. LTE Calling: What's the Difference?

- **Bluetooth Models:** These require your phone to be nearby and connected via Bluetooth. The call is routed through your watch, but it uses your phone's cellular connection.

- **LTE Models:** These are capable of making and receiving calls independently, even when your phone is turned off or out of range. As long as your watch has an active cellular plan with your carrier, it acts as a standalone device for calls and texts.

How to Make a Call from Your Galaxy Watch

There are several ways to initiate a call:

1. **Using the Phone App on the Watch:**
   o Press the **Home button** to access your apps.
   o Tap the **Phone icon**.
   o From here, you can:
      ▪ Browse **Contacts** stored on your watch or synced from your phone.
      ▪ Use the **Dialpad** to enter a number manually.
      ▪ Check **Recents** to call someone you've spoken with recently.

   o Tap the contact or number and press the green **Call** icon to initiate the call.

2. **Using Voice Assistant (Bixby or Google Assistant):**
   o Say, **"Call [Contact Name]"** or **"Dial [Phone Number]"**.
   o The assistant will confirm and place the call automatically.
   o This is particularly useful when your hands are occupied or you're in a hurry.

3. **Using a Watch Face Shortcut or Tile:**
   o Many watch faces support complications (shortcuts) for direct access to contacts or the Phone app.
   o Add a **Call tile** to your swipeable widgets for quicker access.

During the Call:

- **Microphone and Speaker:** Your watch uses its built-in mic and speaker to let you converse hands-free.

- **Volume Control:** Tap the volume icon or use on-screen buttons to adjust audio levels.

- **Mute Mic:** Tap the microphone icon if you need to mute your voice temporarily.

- **Switch to Phone:** If you want to continue the call on your smartphone, just tap **"Switch to phone"** and pick up where you left off.

Answering Calls on the Watch:

- When a call comes in, your watch will **ring or vibrate**, depending on your sound settings.

- You'll see the caller's name or number on the screen.

- **Swipe up** or tap the green phone icon to answer.

- **Swipe down** or tap the red phone icon to decline.

- You can also answer or reject a call using the **physical buttons**—press the **Home button** to answer, or the **Back button** to reject.

Call Settings and Tips:

- To **change the ringtone**, go to **Settings > Sounds and Vibration > Ringtone**.

- Enable **vibration-only mode** during workouts or quiet environments.

- Turn on **Call Forwarding** (for LTE models) if you want missed calls routed to your phone when out of signal range.

When Paired with Bluetooth Headphones:

- The call audio can be automatically routed through your Galaxy Buds or other paired Bluetooth earbuds.
- Great for privacy and better sound quality in public spaces.

Quick Replies and Voice Typing for Messages

In addition to handling calls, your Galaxy Watch makes responding to texts, emails, and instant messages fast and effortless. The watch provides multiple input options—so whether you're in a meeting, walking, or driving, you can stay in touch without reaching for your phone.

How to View and Open Messages:

- **Swipe right** from the main watch face to access the Notification panel.
- Tap any message to open it in full view.
- Scroll to read the entire message and see options to respond.

Replying Options:

Samsung has built several intuitive ways to reply to messages—giving you control over how detailed or quick your responses are.

1. Quick Replies (Pre-Set Messages)

These are short, common responses you can send with just a tap. Examples include:

- "OK"
- "I'll call you later"
- "Can't talk now"
- "Thanks!"

To Use a Quick Reply:

- Open the message.
- Tap **Reply**.
- Choose from the list of pre-written responses.

To Customize Quick Replies:

- Open the **Galaxy Wearable** app on your phone.
- Go to **Watch Settings > Notifications > Quick Responses**.
- Edit existing replies or add new ones based on your usual conversations.

Tip: You can create replies for different tones—professional, casual, or humorous—so you're always ready with the right words.

2. Voice Typing (Voice-to-Text Dictation)

Perfect when your hands are full, or you're walking:

- Tap the **microphone icon**.
- Speak naturally and clearly.
- Your speech is transcribed into text instantly.
- Review the message before hitting **Send**.

Voice typing is accurate and fast in quiet settings. You can speak in complete sentences or short phrases, and it works for texts, WhatsApp messages, emails, and more.

3. On-Screen Keyboard

When you need a custom or detailed message and voice input isn't ideal:

- Tap the **keyboard icon**.
- Use either:
    - **Tap typing** (letter by letter), or
    - **Swipe typing** (slide your finger across letters)

- Autocorrect and predictive suggestions make it easier to type quickly.

Though the keyboard is small, it's surprisingly functional—especially with practice.

4. Emoji Responses

Sometimes an emoji says it all.

- Tap the **emoji icon** to open the emoji panel.
- Browse by category or recent emojis.
- Tap to send.

Useful for casual replies, especially on messaging apps like WhatsApp or Telegram.

5. Handwriting (Draw Letters with Your Finger)

Available on select models and watch faces:

- Tap the **pen icon** when replying.
- Use your finger to write one letter at a time.
- The watch converts your handwriting into text.

While slower than typing or dictation, this method offers more privacy in quiet or professional settings.

Messaging Tips:

- If using multiple messaging apps (e.g., WhatsApp, Telegram, Messages), you can select which ones send notifications to your watch via the Galaxy Wearable app.

- Turn on **Smart Reply suggestions** for AI-generated responses based on message content.

- Use **"Reply Later"** if you need time to respond and don't want to forget the message.

Customizing Notifications to Suit Your Lifestyle

With smart notification management, you can control exactly what shows up on your wrist, when it arrives, and how it alerts you. Whether you want to stay connected 24/7 or prefer a quieter, distraction-free experience, the Galaxy Watch gives you the tools to tailor your notifications to your lifestyle.

How Notification Sync Works

By default, your watch mirrors most notifications from your phone. Whenever you receive a call, text, calendar reminder, email, or app alert, it appears on your watch in real time. This seamless syncing ensures you never miss something important—even if your phone is in your pocket, bag, or across the room.

However, not all notifications are equal—and not all are welcome on your wrist. That's where customization comes in.

Customizing Notification Settings on the Watch

To fine-tune notifications directly from the watch:

1. Go to **Settings > Notifications**
2. Toggle **Notifications** on or off entirely
3. Scroll through your installed apps and enable or disable individual ones
   - For example, keep **Messages**, **Calls**, and **Calendar** active
   - Disable apps like **Promotional Offers**, **Social Games**, or **Shopping Alerts**

You can also adjust how notifications appear:

- **Show While Using Phone**: Decide if alerts should display on your watch when your phone is actively in use
- **Notification Preview**: Show full message content or just a summary
- **Sound and Vibration**: Choose between tones, vibration, or silent modes for each alert

Using the Galaxy Wearable App for Deeper Customization

For a broader view and easier control, use the **Galaxy Wearable** app:

1. Open the app and tap **Watch Settings > Notifications**
2. Toggle **"Show phone notifications on watch"**
3. Select how notifications are delivered:
   - **Show alerts when phone not in use**
   - **Show all notifications**
   - **Mute notifications when wearing watch**

4. Tap **"More" or "App Notifications"** to enable or disable alerts for specific apps

You can also access **Quick Replies** customization here and add or remove pre-written responses for messaging apps.

Creating a Notification Experience That Fits Your Life

Here are some tips to personalize your experience based on your routine:

For Workdays:

- Enable calendar, email, and messaging apps
- Mute social media and games
- Turn on Do Not Disturb during meetings (or schedule it)

For Workouts or Outdoor Activities:

- Enable fitness tracking, music control, and emergency alerts
- Silence non-essential apps
- Use vibration-only mode for subtle feedback

For Downtime and Sleep:

- Use **Bedtime Mode** to silence all alerts except alarms and health tracking
- Schedule **Do Not Disturb** to activate automatically at night
- Keep sleep tracking on, but mute calls and texts

For Travel or Commutes:

- Enable maps, reminders, and weather alerts
- Turn on notifications for transportation apps (like Uber or transit)

- Use LTE (if supported) to stay connected when away from your phone

Smart Features to Reduce Distractions

Your Galaxy Watch offers built-in tools to help manage digital noise:

- **Do Not Disturb**: Blocks all alerts during designated times or manually
- **Theater Mode**: Silences sound and disables the screen from waking
- **Focus Mode (via connected Samsung phone)**: Temporarily mutes selected apps on both phone and watch
- **Mute Connected Phone**: When the watch is worn, you can silence your phone to keep alerts wrist-only

Notification Icons and What They Mean

Each app shows a distinct icon next to its alert—messages, email, calls, health, and third-party apps all have identifiable symbols so you can glance and decide if it needs immediate attention.

You can **swipe down** to clear all notifications or **tap and hold** any notification to access app-specific settings and mute it directly from the watch.

Chapter 4

Monitoring Your Health and Wellness

Understanding Health Tracking Features

Powered by cutting-edge biosensors and Samsung Health's intelligent software, Galaxy Watch 7 Series provides continuous insights into your body, helping you make better lifestyle decisions, track fitness progress, manage stress, and even detect early signs of potential health issues. What sets the Galaxy Watch 7 Series apart is how seamlessly it integrates this data into your daily life, giving you actionable feedback in real time without overwhelming you with information.

A Holistic Approach to Health Monitoring

Here's a breakdown of the key wellness features built into your Galaxy Watch 7 Series:

- **24/7 Heart Rate Monitoring**: Automatically tracks your heart's activity, detects abnormalities, and gives you a window into your cardiovascular health.

- **Electrocardiogram (ECG)**: Captures your heart's electrical activity to screen for arrhythmias like atrial fibrillation.

- **Irregular Heart Rhythm Notification (IHRN)**: Monitors for irregular patterns passively and alerts you if anything unusual is detected.

- **Blood Oxygen (SpO$_2$) Monitoring**: Measures how well oxygen is being distributed in your blood—critical for workouts, sleep, and respiratory awareness.

- **Body Composition Analysis**: Gives you metrics like body fat percentage, muscle mass, BMI, and water retention—all in under a minute.

- **Sleep Tracking and Coaching**: Monitors your sleep cycles, snoring, oxygen levels during rest, and provides personalized tips for improving sleep quality.

- **Stress Management**: Detects high-stress levels based on heart rate variability and offers guided breathing sessions to help you calm down.

- **Skin Temperature Sensor**: Captures subtle changes in your body temperature, especially useful for sleep monitoring and cycle tracking.

- **Women's Health Tools**: Supports menstrual tracking, fertility prediction, and hormone phase awareness.

All this data syncs to your **Samsung Health** app, where it's organized into clear, easy-to-read graphs. You can view trends over days, weeks, and months to better understand your body's patterns and progress.

Tracking Heart Rate and Cardiac Health

Heart health is the foundation of your overall wellness, and the Galaxy Watch 7 Series treats it with the importance it deserves. Using a high-precision **optical heart rate sensor**, your watch delivers continuous and accurate heart rate readings throughout the day and night. Whether you're at rest, exercising, or experiencing a stressful situation, your Galaxy Watch keeps a pulse on how your heart is responding.

Real-Time Heart Rate Monitoring

Your watch automatically checks your heart rate at regular intervals or continuously, depending on your chosen setting.

To manually measure your heart rate:

1. Swipe to the **Heart Rate** tile on your watch or open the Samsung Health app.
2. Tap **Measure** to initiate a reading.
3. Wait a few seconds while the sensor analyzes your pulse.
4. Your result will appear in beats per minute (BPM), along with a short message indicating whether it's in a normal range for your current state (resting, active, etc.).

You can review past heart rate data in your **Samsung Health** app under **Heart Rate**, where it's broken down by time of day, activity, and even sleep period.

Continuous Monitoring Settings

To adjust heart rate tracking frequency:

- On your watch, go to **Samsung Health** > **Settings** > **Heart Rate Monitoring**
- Choose one of the following:

- ○ **Measure continuously** (best for detailed health tracking and stress detection)
- ○ **Every 10 minutes while still** (conserves battery life)
- ○ **Manual only** (you decide when to check)

While continuous tracking uses slightly more battery, it enables features like automatic stress detection and enhanced sleep analysis.

Irregular Heart Rhythm Notifications (IHRN)

Your Galaxy Watch continuously monitors your heart rhythm in the background while you're still. If it detects signs of **atrial fibrillation (AFib)**—a common but serious heart condition—it sends an alert advising you to take further action.

- This feature runs passively, with no user input required.
- If irregular patterns are detected repeatedly, you'll be prompted to take an **ECG reading**.

This function is particularly valuable for users who may have undiagnosed cardiac conditions or a family history of heart problems.

Electrocardiogram (ECG) Functionality

The built-in ECG sensor records the electrical signals from your heart, creating a graph similar to what you'd get in a clinic.

To take an ECG:

1. Open the **Samsung Health Monitor** app on your watch (available on Samsung phones only).

2. Sit down, relax your arms, and rest your finger gently on the **Home button** (upper button) for 30 seconds.

3. The watch will capture your heart rhythm and display whether it's a **normal sinus rhythm** or **signs of AFib**.

4. Results are saved to the app, and you can **export them as a PDF** to share with your healthcare provider.

Note: ECG features may require regulatory approval in your region and are only available when the watch is paired with a Samsung Galaxy phone.

Heart Rate Alerts

Your watch can automatically alert you when your heart rate is abnormally high or low while at rest.

To enable alerts:

- Open **Samsung Health > Heart Rate > Settings > Heart Rate Alerts**
- Set custom thresholds (e.g., **Above 120 BPM** or **Below 50 BPM**)

If your BPM goes beyond these limits for a sustained period, the watch will vibrate and show a warning, prompting you to rest or seek medical attention.

Best Practices for Accurate Heart Monitoring

- **Wear the watch snugly**—not too tight, not too loose. The sensor must sit flat against your skin, just above the wrist bone.

- **Avoid measuring while moving**, especially during vigorous arm motions or talking.

- **Clean the sensors regularly** with a soft, lint-free cloth to avoid interference from sweat, lotions, or dust.

- **Keep the watch charged**, as heart rate monitoring can be affected by power-saving mode if battery levels are low.

Why Heart Monitoring Matters

Heart rate data can reveal a lot about your physical and emotional state. By keeping a close eye on your heart, you can:

- Track your **fitness improvements**—a lower resting heart rate often reflects improved cardiovascular conditioning.
- Understand your **body's stress signals**, even before you feel overwhelmed.
- Spot early warning signs of **cardiac irregularities**, like AFib or tachycardia.
- Monitor **recovery time** after workouts or illness.
- Make **data-driven lifestyle choices**—from hydration and sleep quality to workout intensity and stress management.

Checking Your Blood Oxygen (SpO$_2$) Levels

Monitoring your blood oxygen saturation—or **SpO$_2$**—gives you valuable insight into how well your body is distributing oxygen to your organs and muscles. This is particularly important during physical activity, sleep, high altitudes, or when managing respiratory conditions. The Galaxy Watch 7 Series includes a **dedicated SpO$_2$ sensor** that allows you to check your levels on-demand or track them automatically during sleep.

What is SpO$_2$ and Why It Matters

SpO$_2$ represents the **percentage of oxygen-saturated hemoglobin** relative to the total hemoglobin in your blood. A healthy SpO$_2$ level typically falls between **95% and 100%**. Anything below 90% may signal oxygen deficiency, known as hypoxemia, which can lead to fatigue, headaches, shortness of breath, or more serious health risks—especially if sustained.

Low SpO$_2$ levels may indicate:

- Poor respiratory function
- Sleep apnea
- Altitude sickness
- Poor blood circulation
- Cardiovascular conditions

The Galaxy Watch helps you stay ahead of these risks with fast and non-invasive measurement.

How to Manually Check SpO$_2$ on Your Galaxy Watch

1. From the main watch face, swipe left or open the **Samsung Health** app.
2. Scroll down and tap **Blood Oxygen**.
3. Tap **Measure**.

4. Sit still, keep your watch snug against your wrist, and rest your arm on a flat surface during the scan.

5. After about 15–30 seconds, your SpO_2 level will be displayed.

Important Tips for Accuracy:

- Perform the test **while seated and at rest**—movement disrupts readings.
- Make sure the **watch is clean and fitted correctly**.
- Avoid strong light exposure (e.g., direct sunlight) during testing.
- Do not talk or move your hand during the scan.

Results will be displayed immediately and logged in the **Samsung Health app**, where you can track long-term trends.

SpO_2 Monitoring During Sleep

For deeper health insights, the Galaxy Watch also **monitors SpO_2 automatically during sleep**—helping detect oxygen dips linked to conditions like **sleep apnea** or **nocturnal asthma**.

To enable this feature:

1. Open the **Samsung Health** app on your phone.
2. Go to **Sleep > Settings > Blood Oxygen During Sleep**.
3. Toggle it **on**.

The watch will now monitor your oxygen levels while you sleep and include the data in your sleep report the next morning. You'll see a graph showing fluctuations throughout the night and a summary of your lowest and average SpO_2 values.

Note: Consistently low SpO_2 during sleep may indicate interrupted breathing patterns. If your levels dip below 90% regularly, it may be worth discussing with your healthcare provider.

How SpO_2 Supports Fitness and Altitude Acclimation

If you engage in **intense cardio workouts**, high-altitude activities, or endurance training, checking your blood oxygen levels can help you determine whether your body is adapting properly. Athletes often use SpO_2 data to:

- Monitor **aerobic efficiency**
- Assess **recovery post-exercise**
- Prevent overtraining or fatigue
- Track adaptation to **altitude or low-oxygen environments**

When SpO_2 drops significantly during or after a workout, it's a sign to rest, hydrate, or adjust your training intensity.

Limitations and Considerations

- SpO_2 measurements on smartwatches are intended for **wellness and fitness**—not clinical diagnosis.
- Measurements may be less accurate for users with tattoos, darker skin tones, or poor circulation.
- The feature should not be used as a replacement for professional medical equipment or advice.

Still, when used consistently and correctly, SpO_2 tracking can become a powerful tool in your health-monitoring routine.

Body Composition: What It Means and How to Track

Another groundbreaking feature in the Galaxy Watch 7 Series is **body composition analysis**. Using Samsung's **BioActive Sensor**, your watch can provide insights into key fitness metrics like **body fat percentage, skeletal muscle mass, basal metabolic rate (BMR), BMI**, and **total body water**—in under 30 seconds. This kind of data was once only available through specialized gym equipment, but now it's accessible right on your wrist.

What is Body Composition?

Your **body composition** is the ratio of different components that make up your body—such as fat, muscle, bone, and water. Understanding these metrics gives you a more complete picture of your fitness than weight alone.

Here's what your Galaxy Watch measures:

- **Body Fat (%)**: The percentage of fat in your body compared to everything else (muscle, bones, organs, water).

- **Skeletal Muscle Mass**: The weight of your muscles attached to the skeleton, vital for strength and mobility.

- **Body Water (%)**: Your body's hydration level—important for overall health, recovery, and metabolism.

- **BMI (Body Mass Index)**: A general indicator comparing weight to height.

- **Basal Metabolic Rate (BMR)**: The number of calories your body needs to perform basic functions at rest.

How to Take a Body Composition Measurement

1. **Go to Samsung Health** on your watch and tap **Body Composition**.

2. Follow the on-screen instructions.
   - **Remove any accessories** like rings or metal bracelets.
   - Ensure your watch fits **snugly**, just above your wrist bone.

3. **Place your middle and ring fingers** on the **two side buttons** (they act as electrodes). Do not press the buttons—just rest your fingers lightly.

4. **Hold still** and keep your arms raised away from your body for about 20–30 seconds.

5. Once complete, the watch will display your results.

All results are stored in the **Samsung Health app**, where you can view progress over time, set fitness goals, and compare readings.

Why Body Composition is More Valuable than Weight Alone

While weight gives you a general number, it doesn't tell you **what that weight is made of**. Two people can weigh the same, but have very different fat-to-muscle ratios. Body composition tells you:

- If your training is building muscle

- Whether your weight loss is healthy (fat loss vs. muscle loss)
- If you're hydrated properly
- How your metabolism is responding to activity and diet

This is especially helpful for:

- **Fitness enthusiasts and athletes** tracking performance
- **Individuals managing weight loss or muscle gain**
- **Anyone recovering from illness or injury** and monitoring muscle retention
- **People managing lifestyle-related conditions** like diabetes or obesity

Interpreting Your Results

You'll receive a comprehensive breakdown of each metric, along with helpful context from Samsung Health. Green markers indicate healthy ranges based on age, gender, and body type. You can set goals (e.g., reduce body fat by 3%) and track weekly or monthly progress charts.

If you're not within ideal ranges, don't worry. The purpose of this tool is to inform, not to judge. With regular tracking, you can use small changes in your routine—like diet, hydration, exercise, or sleep—to guide long-term improvement.

Body Composition Best Practices

- Take measurements at the **same time of day**, ideally in the morning, before meals or exercise
- **Remove metal jewelry** and ensure your skin is dry
- Avoid measuring if you've just exercised, eaten, or consumed caffeine or alcohol

- Wear the watch on your **non-dominant wrist** for consistency
- Stay **hydrated**, as dehydration can affect results

Better Sleep Insights with Advanced Sleep Coaching

Sleep isn't just rest—it's a biological necessity that affects your physical recovery, cognitive function, and emotional well-being. With the Galaxy Watch 7 Series, Samsung has taken sleep tracking to a deeper level by integrating real-time monitoring with personalized coaching tools that guide you toward healthier sleep habits. The watch doesn't just measure how long you sleep; it analyzes how well you sleep, detects disturbances, and provides actionable recommendations to improve your nightly rest.

What Your Watch Tracks While You Sleep

As you wear your Galaxy Watch overnight, it uses a combination of sensors—including heart rate, blood oxygen, motion detection, and skin temperature—to monitor your sleep with precision. The watch captures:

- Sleep duration and total time asleep
- Sleep stages (light, deep, REM) and how much time you spend in each
- Sleep consistency over multiple nights
- Wake times and interruptions
- Blood oxygen levels (SpO_2) throughout the night
- Snoring (if your paired phone is placed nearby with the microphone enabled)
- Skin temperature variation during sleep

These data points are collected seamlessly and presented in a comprehensive morning report inside the Samsung Health app, allowing you to see how your night unfolded.

How to Enable Sleep Tracking

1. Ensure your watch is securely fitted and worn during sleep.
2. Open the Samsung Health app on your phone.
3. Tap **Sleep**, then **Settings**.
4. Enable options like **Blood Oxygen During Sleep**, **Snore Detection**, and **Skin Temperature Monitoring**.
5. Optionally, place your phone near your pillow with the microphone facing you to record snoring.

Understanding Your Sleep Score

Each morning, you'll receive a **Sleep Score** based on the quality of your rest. This score is calculated from your sleep duration, sleep cycles, movement, oxygen levels, and interruptions. A high score reflects uninterrupted, restorative sleep, while a lower score indicates potential disruptions or insufficient rest.

Advanced Sleep Coaching

Samsung takes it a step further by offering **Advanced Sleep Coaching**, a personalized program that uses your sleep data over 7 consecutive nights to create a tailored action plan. After your first week of tracking, the system assigns you a **Sleep Animal**, a symbolic representation of your sleep type (e.g., Nervous Penguin, Easygoing Lion). This makes the experience relatable and more engaging.

- Setting consistent sleep and wake times
- Adjusting evening routines to limit screen time or caffeine
- Creating a wind-down ritual
- Establishing an ideal sleep environment
- Practicing breathing or mindfulness before bed

The program evolves with you. As you improve your sleep behavior, the watch continues to adapt and refine your guidance.

Benefits of Long-Term Sleep Tracking

By monitoring your sleep consistently, you can:

- Identify patterns that affect your energy levels
- Understand how stress, activity, and diet impact your rest
- Detect potential issues like sleep apnea or poor oxygenation
- Receive gentle nudges to adopt better sleep hygiene
- Improve focus, mood, immunity, and overall health

Managing Stress with Breathing Exercises

Modern life comes with its share of stress, and the Galaxy Watch 7 Series is designed to help you manage it proactively. With built-in stress tracking and guided breathing tools, the watch empowers you to slow down, reset your mind, and build emotional resilience—right from your wrist.

How the Watch Detects Stress

The watch uses your **heart rate variability (HRV)**—the variation in time between heartbeats—as a marker of stress. When you're tense or anxious, HRV typically decreases, signaling your body is in fight-or-flight mode. The Galaxy Watch continuously tracks this data and calculates a **Stress Score**.

You can check your current stress level at any time by:

1. Swiping to the **Stress** tile on your watch
2. Viewing a visual scale (usually color-coded: blue for low, yellow for moderate, red for high)
3. Seeing a breakdown of your recent stress trends in the Samsung Health app

Setting Up Continuous Stress Monitoring

1. Open the Samsung Health app on your phone
2. Go to **Stress > Settings**
3. Enable **Measure continuously** for passive background tracking
4. Make sure your watch is snug on your wrist and worn throughout the day

Using Breathing Exercises to Manage Stress

When your stress level is elevated, the watch will often recommend a **guided breathing session** to help you relax. You can also access it anytime by opening the **Samsung Health > Breathe** option on the watch.

Here's how a typical session works:

1. Choose a session length (usually 1, 2, or 5 minutes)
2. Sit comfortably and relax your arms
3. Follow the on-screen animation and vibration cues

4. Inhale and exhale slowly in sync with the visual guide

5. At the end, the watch will show your post-session heart rate and a stress level comparison

This simple practice has proven benefits for:

- Lowering heart rate and blood pressure
- Reducing muscle tension
- Improving focus and mood
- Increasing emotional awareness and regulation

Customizing Breathing Sessions

- Adjust session length in the **Settings** tab of the Breathe app
- Choose between vibration or visual-only guidance
- Pair with ambient music using your connected earbuds for a deeper experience

Daily Mindfulness Through Samsung Health

Beyond reactive stress relief, Samsung Health offers a **Mindfulness section** that includes:

- Meditation sessions
- Sleep sounds and ambient music
- Emotional journaling features (in some regions)
- Headspace content (varies by country)

You can access this content through the Samsung Health app on your phone, and some meditation programs can be synced for playback on your watch.

Tracking Stress Over Time

The Samsung Health app displays a daily, weekly, and monthly view of your stress levels, helping you:

- Spot trends linked to work, lifestyle, or habits
- Identify triggers (e.g., caffeine, lack of sleep, overtraining)
- Create a long-term plan for mental and emotional well-being

Encouraging Habits That Reduce Stress

- Schedule regular breathing breaks throughout your day
- Use **Do Not Disturb** mode during peak stress periods
- Set **reminders for mindfulness or walking breaks**
- Combine stress tracking with **sleep insights**, as poor sleep often increases tension

Women's Health and Cycle Tracking

The Galaxy Watch 7 Series includes comprehensive women's health tools that help you track your menstrual cycle, understand hormonal patterns, and monitor symptoms with greater accuracy. Whether you're managing your fertility, navigating symptoms of PMS, or simply staying informed about your body's natural rhythm, these features are designed to give you more control and awareness—all directly from your wrist.

Cycle Tracking Through Samsung Health

The menstrual tracking feature is integrated into the Samsung Health app and works seamlessly with your Galaxy Watch. It allows you to log cycle dates, track symptoms, receive period predictions, and get insights into your reproductive health.

To begin using it:

1. Open the **Samsung Health** app on your phone
2. Scroll down and tap **Women's Health**
3. Tap **Start tracking your cycle**
4. Enter your last period's start and end dates, along with your average cycle length
5. Enable **Cycle Notifications** to receive period predictions, fertile window alerts, and symptom reminders on your watch

Once setup is complete, the watch and app work together to display your current phase (menstrual, fertile, ovulation, or luteal), give you calendar-based forecasts, and allow you to log daily data for better accuracy over time.

Logging Symptoms and Notes

You can log a variety of physical and emotional symptoms that occur throughout your cycle:

- Cramps
- Mood swings
- Bloating
- Acne
- Headaches
- Breast tenderness

- Energy levels
- Discharge type

You can also add notes to track additional observations, lifestyle changes, or medical treatments.

All this data helps the app better predict your cycle and ovulation timing with improved precision. The more consistently you log symptoms and cycle details, the smarter and more accurate the tracking becomes.

Fertility and Ovulation Tracking

If you're trying to conceive or simply want to understand your fertility window, Samsung Health provides ovulation predictions based on your cycle history and symptoms. You'll see:

- Upcoming fertile days
- Ovulation day estimate
- Cycle phase overviews
- A complete fertility calendar

The watch can alert you when you're entering your fertile window or ovulation period, offering discreet reminders and empowering you to plan with greater awareness.

Integration with Skin Temperature and Sleep Tracking

The Galaxy Watch 7 Series adds another layer of insight through **skin temperature monitoring** during sleep. Subtle changes in nighttime skin temperature often correspond with ovulation, hormone shifts, or irregularities. This passive data collection can enhance the accuracy of cycle predictions when paired with logged symptoms and sleep patterns.

Over time, your temperature trend may help you:

- Identify cycle irregularities
- Notice signs of early ovulation
- Understand how sleep and hormonal phases interact
- Track hormonal fluctuations during perimenopause or post-pregnancy

Privacy and Discretion

Samsung prioritizes privacy with this feature:

- All health data, including menstrual tracking, is stored securely
- You can enable or disable notifications at any time
- Cycle updates appear discreetly on the watch face or tiles—no one else will know what the alert refers to unless they open the app

Additional Uses for Women of All Ages

While often used for fertility awareness, this tool is also valuable for:

- Monitoring **perimenopausal transitions**
- Managing symptoms related to **PCOS** or **endometriosis**
- Understanding how your **hormones affect your sleep, mood, or workouts**
- Identifying **anomalies** that may require medical consultation

Helpful Tips for Better Accuracy

- Log your period start and end dates regularly

- Record daily symptoms to improve pattern detection
- Use the **"Insights"** section in Samsung Health to view long-term trends
- Pair this data with your physical activity and nutrition tracking for a holistic view of your well-being

Chapter 5

Fitness and Activity Made Simple

Starting and Tracking Workouts

How to Start a Workout Manually

1. From the watch face, press the **Home button** or swipe up to access the app screen.

2. Tap on **Samsung Health**.

3. Scroll to and select **Workout**.

4. Browse or search the list of activities—you'll find over 90 workout types, including:

   o Walking

   o Running (indoor and outdoor)

   o Cycling

   o Swimming

   o Hiking

   o Rowing machine

   o Elliptical trainer

   o Strength training

   o Pilates

   o Yoga

   o Circuit training

   o HIIT

   o Custom workouts

5. Tap your chosen workout, then press **Start**.

6. Your watch will begin tracking metrics like:
    - Duration
    - Calories burned
    - Distance (for applicable activities)
    - Heart rate zones
    - Speed/pace
    - Repetitions (for weight training)
    - Elevation gain (for hiking and outdoor runs)
    - VO_2 max (for intense cardio workouts)

During Your Workout

- The watch display shows live metrics in real time

- You can **pause/resume** your session by pressing the **Back button** or tapping the screen

- Swipe to view different data screens, including your heart rate, time elapsed, or distance

- For activities like running or biking, you can view your pace split by kilometer or mile

- With connected Bluetooth earbuds, you'll receive **audio feedback** for pace and milestones

After Your Workout

- Once you finish, tap **Finish** or press the **Back button**, then confirm

- You'll see a **summary screen** showing all relevant stats for that session

- The data syncs automatically to the **Samsung Health** app on your phone

- In the app, you can view workout history, compare performance over time, and access detailed charts

Setting Workout Goals

You can set goals for each session before starting:

- **Duration** (e.g., 30 minutes)
- **Distance** (e.g., 5 km)
- **Calories burned**
- **Repetition or Set targets** (for strength training)

To set a goal:

1. Tap on a workout
2. Scroll down and select **Set Goal**
3. Choose your desired goal and tap **Done**

You'll receive alerts and feedback as you progress toward your goal during the workout.

Advanced Fitness Features

- **VO₂ Max Tracking**: During outdoor runs, the watch estimates your VO_2 max (the maximum oxygen your body can use), which is a key indicator of aerobic fitness.

- **Running Coach**: Provides real-time coaching, pacing, and form analysis for beginner to advanced runners.

- **Interval Training**: Set up custom intervals of work and rest periods for HIIT or sprint training.

- **Strength Training Auto Reps**: Recognizes certain movements like squats, curls, or bench presses and automatically counts reps for you.

Outdoor Workouts and GPS Tracking

- The Galaxy Watch 7 and Ultra come with built-in **multi-satellite GPS support** (GPS, GLONASS, Galileo, BeiDou) for highly accurate location tracking.

- Ideal for running, hiking, and cycling without your phone

- The **Galaxy Watch Ultra** includes a **track-back feature**, guiding you back to your starting point—perfect for trail runners or backcountry hikers

Automatic Workout Recognition (No More Missed Workouts!)

One of the most convenient fitness features of the Galaxy Watch 7 Series is its ability to recognize certain workouts automatically—so even if you forget to press "Start," your activity still gets logged.

How It Works

Your watch detects patterns of movement that match common exercises. If you walk, run, cycle, or perform another supported activity for a sustained period, it will start tracking in the background.

Supported Auto-Detected Workouts Include:

- Walking
- Running
- Elliptical trainer
- Rowing machine
- Swimming
- Cycling
- Dynamic workouts (general aerobic activity)

Default Recognition Settings

- The watch begins tracking after **about 10 minutes of continuous activity**, though this varies slightly depending on intensity and consistency.

- A notification appears saying **"Workout detected: [Activity]"**, and it begins logging metrics from the start of the session—not just from the moment of detection.

- You can accept the detected workout or let it continue silently in the background.

What Data is Collected Automatically

- Duration
- Steps taken
- Distance (for walking/running/cycling)
- Calories burned
- Heart rate zones
- Elevation and route map (for outdoor activities using GPS)

Adjusting Auto Workout Settings

1. On your watch, go to **Samsung Health > Settings > Auto Detect Workouts**

2. Toggle individual workouts **on or off** based on your preference
3. You can also choose whether to include **GPS tracking** in auto-detected outdoor activities

Benefits of Automatic Recognition

- **Never miss a workout**—even if you forget to tap "Start"
- Seamlessly track **spontaneous activity** like a walk during lunch or an impromptu jog
- Keeps your fitness records more accurate and complete
- Useful for users who prefer **low-maintenance tracking**

Auto-Pause for Running and Cycling

If you stop moving during a workout (e.g., waiting at a red light or resting), the watch can automatically **pause the session** and resume when you start again. This keeps your stats accurate, especially for pace and active time.

You can enable this in:

- **Samsung Health > Running (or Cycling) > Settings > Auto Pause**

Pairing with Fitness Apps and Equipment

- Sync your workout data with **Strava**, **Google Fit**, or **MyFitnessPal** via Samsung Health

- Connect to compatible **gym equipment** using Bluetooth (for treadmills, rowing machines, or bikes with ANT+ or BLE support)

Using GPS for Outdoor Activities (Running, Hiking, Cycling)

The Galaxy Watch 7 Series, especially the Galaxy Watch Ultra, offers precise GPS tracking for a variety of outdoor activities. With integrated support for multiple satellite systems—including GPS, GLONASS, Galileo, and BeiDou—you get fast, accurate location data whether you're running city streets or hiking remote trails. This feature not only maps your route but also enhances your performance tracking with elevation, pace, distance, and split times.

How to Enable GPS for Outdoor Workouts

1. On your watch, open the **Samsung Health** app.

2. Tap **Workout**, then choose an outdoor activity such as **Running**, **Hiking**, or **Cycling**.

3. Ensure that **GPS** is enabled (usually toggled on by default for outdoor workouts).

4. Wait for the watch to acquire a satellite signal—this typically takes a few seconds if you're in an open area.

5. Once the GPS icon turns green or the watch says "GPS connected," press **Start** to begin tracking.

GPS-Enabled Data Captured During Workouts

- Route mapping (viewable in the Samsung Health app)
- Distance traveled
- Real-time pace and split times
- Elevation gain/loss
- Speed variations across different terrain
- VO$_2$ max estimate (for runners, calculated during sustained outdoor runs)

After finishing your session, you can view a detailed workout summary, including a route map with color-coded intensity zones (based on pace or heart rate), total elevation changes, and average speed per mile or kilometer.

Track Back Feature (Galaxy Watch Ultra)

For explorers, the Galaxy Watch Ultra includes a **Track Back** feature—a navigation tool that helps you retrace your steps back to your starting point. It's ideal for:

- Hiking in unfamiliar areas
- Trail running without marked paths

- City exploration without needing a phone

To use Track Back:

1. Start a workout with GPS enabled (like **Hiking** or **Walking**).
2. During or after the activity, swipe to the navigation panel.
3. Tap **Track Back** to begin guidance.
4. Follow the on-screen directions and breadcrumb trail back to where you started.

Tips for Accurate GPS Tracking

- Use the watch **in open areas** away from tall buildings or dense tree cover for faster satellite lock.
- Wear the watch on your **outer wrist** with a snug fit—avoid letting it slide.
- If possible, **wait for GPS to fully connect** before starting your workout.
- Enable **auto-pause** if you expect frequent stops (e.g., at traffic lights).
- Turn on **Always-on Display** during workouts for constant visibility of pace and distance.

Using Maps and Navigation Apps

You can enhance your GPS workouts with third-party apps like:

- **Komoot** for route planning and guided navigation
- **Strava** for segment tracking and social sharing
- **Google Maps** (limited interaction, view-only support)

Some apps may require pairing via your phone or downloading through the Galaxy Store before syncing routes to your watch.

Swim Tracking and Water-Resistance Tips

The Galaxy Watch 7 Series is built for more than land-based workouts—it's also a capable swim tracker, designed to withstand water-based training sessions in pools and open water. With **5ATM water resistance** and **IP68 certification**, your watch is safe for laps, aquatic fitness, and even light snorkeling.

Starting a Swim Workout

1. Open the **Samsung Health** app on your watch.
2. Tap **Workout > Swimming**.
3. Choose **Pool Swim** or **Open Water Swim**, depending on your location.
4. Before starting, you can customize:
     - Pool length (for accurate lap count)
     - Workout goal (time, distance, or calorie burn)
     - Stroke recognition and lap alerts (optional)

5. Tap **Start** and begin your swim. The watch will automatically detect your strokes and count laps.

Metrics Tracked During Swim Workouts

- Total laps and distance
- Stroke type (freestyle, breaststroke, backstroke, butterfly)
- Average pace per lap
- SWOLF (Swim Golf) score, a measure of efficiency
- Duration and rest time
- Heart rate (measured during rest intervals for better accuracy)
- Calorie burn

All data syncs with Samsung Health, where you can compare performance across sessions and track improvements over time.

Tips for Accurate Swim Tracking

- Set the correct **pool length** before pool workouts (typically 25m or 50m).
- Wear the watch **tight enough** to prevent movement during strokes.
- Allow the watch to **adjust to water temperature** before starting the session.
- Avoid excessive water turbulence near jets or waterfalls during open water swims.
- Rinse your watch with **freshwater** after swimming to remove chlorine or salt residue.

Understanding Water Lock Mode

When you begin a swim workout, the watch automatically activates **Water Lock Mode**. This mode:

- Disables the touch screen to prevent accidental taps from water contact
- Locks buttons
- Prevents notifications and interactions during your swim
- Enables a water-ejection mechanism (similar to an audio pulse) to clear speaker ports after exiting water

To turn Water Lock Mode on or off manually:

1. Swipe down from the watch face to open **Quick Settings**
2. Tap the **water droplet icon**
3. To exit, press and hold the **Home button** until you hear a tone and feel a vibration (this ejects any trapped water)

Water Resistance Best Practices

- The watch is rated **5ATM**: safe up to 50 meters deep in still water
- Avoid **high-velocity water**, like diving, water skiing, or power showers
- Do not expose the watch to **soap, detergent, or hot water**, which can compromise seals
- Rinse with clean water and dry thoroughly after every swim

Swim Data in Samsung Health

Post-swim, you can review your session in the Samsung Health app with detailed charts on:

- Lap-by-lap performance
- Stroke breakdown
- Rest intervals and heart rate zones
- Weekly summaries for swim duration and efficiency

Daily Activity: Steps, Calories, and More

Your Galaxy Watch 7 Series keeps constant track of your daily movement, ensuring that even small efforts—like taking the stairs or walking your dog—are recognized and recorded. This all-day activity tracking is foundational to understanding how active you are outside of structured workouts. By capturing steps, calories burned, floors climbed, and active minutes, your watch provides a full picture of your baseline physical activity throughout the day.

Steps and Movement Tracking

Your watch uses an integrated accelerometer and gyroscope to count each step you take. These steps are logged automatically, with no need to start a workout. The Galaxy Watch measures:

- **Total daily steps**
- **Hourly step activity**
- **Idle time** and reminders to move if you've been inactive for long periods
- **Step streaks** and consistency over days, weeks, and months

To view your step data:

1. Swipe left on the watch face to access the **Steps widget**
2. Tap the tile for a full overview, including hourly breakdown and trends
3. Open the **Samsung Health** app on your phone to view detailed graphs, averages, and step history

Calorie Burn

Your Galaxy Watch calculates two types of calories:

- **Active calories**: Burned during physical activity like walking, workouts, or chores
- **Total calories**: Includes active calories plus your **Basal Metabolic Rate (BMR)**—the energy your body uses for basic functions like breathing and digestion

These calculations are based on your personalized health profile, which includes:

- Age
- Sex

- Height
- Weight
- Heart rate data
- Type and intensity of physical activity

You can view calories burned:

- In the **Daily Activity** tile on your watch
- In the **Samsung Health** app under **Calories** or **Activities**
- Per workout, broken down by duration and type of movement

Active Time and Intensity

The Galaxy Watch tracks **active minutes** throughout the day. To qualify, movements must be of moderate or high intensity, like brisk walking or climbing stairs. You'll see a ring or progress bar filling up as you reach your daily activity target.

You can view this data in the **Samsung Health** app under **Activity > Active Time**, where your movement is broken into low, moderate, and high intensity zones. It also shows your most active times of the day.

Floors Climbed

Thanks to the built-in barometric altimeter, your watch also tracks **floors climbed** throughout the day. Every time you ascend approximately 3 meters (10 feet), it counts as one floor. This is especially helpful for users looking to improve cardio health or add more vertical movement to their routine.

Idle Time Alerts

If you've been inactive for over an hour, your watch gives you a gentle nudge to move. These **Inactivity Alerts** encourage you to stretch, take a few steps, or complete a one-minute activity to reset the clock. You can customize these alerts or turn them off in the **Settings > Samsung Health > Notifications**.

Daily Activity Summary

Your watch summarizes your daily movement using three key circles or metrics:

1. **Steps**
2. **Active Minutes**
3. **Calorie Burn**

These are visible in the **Daily Activity** tile or through custom watch faces that display real-time stats. The goal is to close your rings each day by staying consistently active, promoting heart health, mobility, and metabolic function.

Setting Realistic Fitness Goals and Tracking Progress

Setting and achieving fitness goals is one of the most powerful ways to stay motivated. Your Galaxy Watch 7 Series, paired with Samsung Health, helps you set goals that are meaningful, attainable, and personalized to your needs—whether you're just starting your fitness journey or training for a marathon.

Setting Your Goals

To set or adjust your daily activity goals:

1. Open the **Samsung Health** app on your phone
2. Tap **Activity**
3. Tap the **three-dot menu** (⋮) and choose **Set targets**

4. Choose daily targets for:

- ○ **Steps** (e.g., 7,000, 10,000, or more)
- ○ **Calories burned**
- ○ **Active minutes**
- ○ **Workout sessions per week**

You can also set **weekly goals** based on your activity history, weight loss objectives, or personal health needs.

For individual workouts, you can set:

- **Time goals** (e.g., 30-minute runs)
- **Distance goals** (e.g., 5K or 10K)
- **Calorie targets**
- **Heart rate zones**

These can be configured directly on your watch before you start each workout.

Viewing Your Progress

Daily, weekly, and monthly overviews help you visualize how you're doing. On your watch, you can:

- Check the **Daily Activity** tile to see real-time progress
- View **Achievements** and streaks, which reward consistent effort
- Access weekly summaries every Sunday evening

In the Samsung Health app on your phone, you can explore:

- Detailed **trend graphs** for each goal
- **Activity history** per day, week, or month

- **Comparison tools** to track improvement over time
- Integration with **weight and body composition goals** (if enabled)

Smart Coaching and Adaptive Goals

Your Galaxy Watch can automatically **adjust your goals** based on recent activity. For example, if you consistently exceed your daily steps, it may recommend increasing your goal to keep you challenged. If you're falling behind, it may suggest reducing goals to maintain motivation.

Fitness Programs and Challenges

To add structure and variety to your goals, Samsung Health also offers:

- **Guided fitness programs**: These include beginner walking routines, weight loss programs, and strength workouts.
- **Step Challenges**: Compete with friends or global users to see who walks the most in a day or week.
- **Community support**: Join fitness groups or share your results for accountability.

Using Milestones and Rewards

Samsung Health provides **badges and achievements** for:

- Reaching new step records
- Completing streaks (e.g., 7 days of 10,000 steps)
- Burning a milestone number of calories
- Achieving a personal best in workouts

These gamified elements encourage consistency and celebrate your progress.

Tips for Reaching Your Goals

- Break large goals into smaller chunks throughout the day
- Use **auto workout detection** to ensure every movement is counted
- Take brief walks during breaks or calls
- Use **idle reminders** as motivation to move
- Mix in a variety of activities—steps aren't just walking; they count from all types of movement
- Sync your Galaxy Watch with third-party apps like Strava or MyFitnessPal to enhance tracking and motivation

Staying Accountable

- Review your stats each morning to plan your activity
- Adjust goals weekly based on your progress and schedule
- Schedule workout alerts or reminders from the Samsung Health app
- Share progress with friends or fitness communities for encouragement

Chapter 6

Boosting Productivity and Fun with Apps

Installing and Managing Apps

With support for the **Google Wear OS** platform, your watch has access to a vast library of apps directly from the **Google Play Store**, optimized for the wrist experience.

Accessing the Google Play Store on Your Watch

You can browse, search for, and install apps directly from your watch without needing your phone:

1. Press the **Home button** to open the app drawer.
2. Tap on the **Play Store** icon.
3. Use the **keyboard**, **voice input**, or **recommended list** to search for apps.
4. Tap an app to see its details, reviews, and size.

5. Tap **Install** to download and install it directly to your watch.
6. After installation, the app appears in your app drawer or as a widget/tile if supported.

You can also browse and install watch-compatible apps using your phone:

1. Open the **Google Play Store** on your smartphone.
2. Search for the app you want.
3. Tap the **down arrow** next to the install button.
4. Select **Galaxy Watch** as the install target.

5. The app will install on your watch automatically.

Managing Installed Apps

Your watch allows you to control which apps remain installed and how they behave:

- *To view installed apps:*
  - Open **Settings > Apps > App list**
  - Scroll through and select an app to adjust its permissions, notifications, or storage

- *To uninstall an app:*
  - Open the **app drawer**
  - Tap and hold the app icon
  - Tap the **"Uninstall"** option or drag it to the trash icon (depending on model)

- *To reorder apps:*
  - Tap and hold an app in the drawer
  - Drag it to your preferred position
  - Customize your layout to keep most-used apps accessible

Managing App Permissions and Background Activity

1. Open **Settings > Apps > App permissions**
2. Choose categories like **Location, Microphone, Sensors**, or **Notifications**
3. Enable or disable access based on what the app needs

You can also control whether an app runs in the background:

- Go to **Settings** > **Battery** > **Background usage limits**
- Choose to **optimize** or **restrict** specific apps to conserve battery

Syncing with Your Phone and Google Account

Apps that work on both your phone and watch (like Keep, Gmail, or Calendar) sync automatically when:

- You are signed into the **same Google account**
- Bluetooth or Wi-Fi/LTE is active
- The app supports cloud sync or account pairing

You can manage sync preferences within each app's settings menu.

Customizing Watch Faces with App Complications

Many apps add **complications** (small widgets) to your watch face for glanceable data:

- Long-press your watch face and tap **Customize**
- Scroll to **Complications** or **Widgets**
- Assign an app (like Weather, Calendar, or Spotify) to that space
- Tap **Save** to activate

Complications let you control music, check schedules, or view fitness stats without opening the full app.

Recommended Apps to Make Life Easier

To get the most out of your Galaxy Watch, loading the right apps can transform your daily routine. Here are top recommended apps across various categories, all compatible with the Galaxy Watch 7 Series and Galaxy Watch Ultra:

Productivity & Time Management

- **Google Calendar** – View your schedule, get event reminders, and set meeting alerts right from your wrist.
- **Google Keep** – Create, view, and edit notes or checklists on the go. Great for grocery lists, reminders, or quick thoughts.
- **Todoist** – A full-featured task manager that syncs with your phone, helping you organize your day and hit deadlines.
- **Microsoft Outlook** – Access and respond to emails, calendar invites, and tasks. Includes quick reply options and notifications.
- **Wear Calendar** – Offers detailed calendar widgets and daily agenda complications with customizable layouts.

Health & Wellness

- **Calm** – Guided meditations, breathing sessions, and relaxing audio for stress relief and focus.
- **Water Reminder** – Logs water intake and reminds you to hydrate based on your activity levels and settings.
- **Pill Reminder & Medication Tracker** – Keeps track of medication schedules with vibration alerts and visual reminders.

- **Google Fit** – Alternative to Samsung Health with similar fitness and wellness tracking, now more deeply integrated with Wear OS.
- **Sleep Cycle** – Advanced sleep monitoring with smart alarm and analysis if you want more depth than Samsung Health offers.

Navigation & Travel

- **Komoot** – Offline maps and route planning for hiking, cycling, and mountain sports. Supports GPX import and elevation maps.
- **Google Maps** – Turn-by-turn navigation, nearby search, and walking/biking directions without needing to look at your phone.
- **Citymapper** – Public transport directions for major cities worldwide—real-time subway, bus, and walking routes.
- **Uber** – Request rides directly from your watch, track arrival time, and view driver details.
- **TripIt** – Keeps your travel plans organized with flight details, hotel bookings, and itinerary notifications on your wrist.

Entertainment & Lifestyle

- **Spotify** – Stream music, podcasts, and playlists, with offline playback support for Premium users.
- **YouTube Music** – Full-featured music player with voice search, recently played items, and offline downloads.
- **Strava** – Track runs, rides, hikes, and sync automatically with your watch for social fitness sharing.
- **Shazam** – Identify music playing around you with a single tap.

- **SmartThings** – Control Samsung-compatible smart home devices (lights, TV, thermostats) directly from your watch.

Utilities & Tools

- **Calculator** – Quick access to basic and scientific calculations.
- **Flashlight App** – Brightens your screen to serve as a temporary flashlight in dark areas.
- **Find My Phone** – Make your phone ring if misplaced, even in silent mode.
- **Voice Recorder** – Record memos, interviews, or quick ideas using your watch's built-in mic.
- **Translate** – Real-time translation of speech and text for international travel or communication.

Fitness & Sport-Specific Tools

- **Nike Run Club** – Guided runs, pace tracking, and coaching built into a sleek and easy-to-use interface.
- **Adidas Running** – Offers real-time stats and integrates with heart rate tracking and social fitness features.
- **Swim.com** – Enhanced swim tracking for serious swimmers and triathletes.
- **Golf Pad** – GPS-based score tracking and club distance analysis for golf courses worldwide.
- **Jump Rope Wear OS** – Tracks jump counts, intervals, and calories for rope-based cardio workouts.

Managing Calendars, Reminders, and Daily Tasks

Syncing Your Calendar

Your watch automatically syncs with your calendar apps when connected to your smartphone. Supported apps include:

- **Google Calendar**
- **Samsung Calendar**
- **Microsoft Outlook** (via the Outlook app)

To set up calendar sync:

1. Ensure your preferred calendar app is installed and logged in on your phone.
2. Open the **Samsung Galaxy Wearable app**.
3. Go to **Watch settings > Accounts and backup > Google account** and ensure your account is linked.
4. Once synced, events from your connected calendars will appear in the **Calendar** app on your watch.

Viewing and Navigating Calendar Events

- Open the **Calendar app** on your watch to see your agenda.
- Use the **rotating bezel** (or swipe gestures) to navigate between days or weeks.
- Tap on a specific day to view event details, including title, time, and location.
- You'll receive **reminders and notifications** directly on your watch face before the event starts.

Setting Reminders

Your Galaxy Watch supports both Google Reminders (via Assistant or Keep) and Samsung's native Reminder app.

To create a reminder:

- Use **Bixby** or **Google Assistant** by saying:
  - "Remind me to call Sarah at 5 PM."
  - "Add a reminder to check the oven in 20 minutes."
- Or manually open the **Reminders** app:
  - Tap + **Add Reminder**
  - Input the title and time using the keyboard or voice-to-text
  - Choose whether it repeats, links to a location, or alerts you at a specific time

Reminders show up as notifications, and you can check them off with a tap once completed.

Managing Tasks with To-Do Apps

If you use structured to-do lists or productivity apps, your Galaxy Watch supports several:

- **Google Keep**: View checklists, notes, and pinned to-dos
- **Todoist**: Access your daily task list, check off items, and receive project updates
- **Microsoft To Do**: With the companion phone app, syncs your tasks and deadlines to the watch

- **TickTick** (if installed on phone): Offers limited support for checking tasks and viewing reminders

Most apps include **complications** for task visibility directly on your watch face, so you can monitor what's next without entering the app.

Setting Alarms and Timers

Your watch has built-in alarm and timer apps, ideal for reminders, wake-up calls, or structured productivity (like Pomodoro technique):

- Open the **Alarm** app to set one-time or repeating alarms
- Open the **Timer** app to set countdowns for tasks or activities
- Use **voice commands** to speed up input:
    - "Set an alarm for 7 AM."
    - "Start a 10-minute timer."

Alarms will vibrate and sound through the speaker, or through your connected earbuds if paired.

Controlling Music and Podcasts Right from Your Wrist

Listening to your favorite music, podcasts, or audiobooks has never been more convenient. Your Galaxy Watch 7 Series and Ultra give you full control over your audio experience, letting you play, pause, skip, adjust volume, and switch tracks directly from your wrist—whether your phone is nearby or you're streaming directly from the watch.

Using the Built-In Music App

The Galaxy Watch includes a native **Samsung Music** app and also supports:

- **Spotify**
- **YouTube Music**
- **Amazon Music**
- **Audible** (for audiobooks, via companion phone sync)
- **Google Podcasts** (with third-party support)

You can play audio through:

- **Your phone's speaker**
- **Bluetooth earbuds** (like Galaxy Buds or others)
- **The watch's built-in speaker** (best for voice or short audio)

Playing Music Stored on the Watch

To add music directly to your watch:

1. Open the **Galaxy Wearable app**
2. Tap **Watch Settings > Manage Content**
3. Select **Add tracks** or **Sync playlists**
4. Choose files from your phone to transfer to your watch

Once synced, you can:

- Open the **Music** app
- Browse by track, album, artist, or playlist
- Shuffle or loop playback
- Control playback even if your phone is out of range

This is ideal for workouts when you want to leave your phone behind.

Streaming Music on the Go

If your watch is connected to Wi-Fi or LTE (Ultra model), you can stream from apps like:

- **Spotify**: Log into your account, browse playlists, albums, or podcasts
  - Premium users can **download music offline** for phone-free playback
- **YouTube Music**: Offers offline downloads and streaming for YouTube Premium members
- **Amazon Music**: Works similarly with downloaded content for Prime Music subscribers

Controlling Playback from Phone

When you're playing music or podcasts on your phone (e.g., Spotify, Apple Music, Audible), your Galaxy Watch acts as a **remote control**:

- Use the **Media Controller widget**
- Play, pause, skip tracks
- Adjust volume
- See track info and album art
- Tap to open the app if deeper controls are needed

This is perfect for commuting, cooking, or running errands with your phone in your bag or pocket.

Managing Podcasts and Audiobooks

- Use **Spotify or YouTube Music** for podcast streaming
- For audiobooks, use **Audible** with synced content from your phone
- Control chapter navigation, playback speed, and bookmarks from your watch screen

- Pair with **Bluetooth headphones** for hands-free listening while working out or multitasking

Voice Commands for Audio Control

Activate **Bixby** or **Google Assistant** to control music:

- "Play my workout playlist on Spotify."
- "Skip this track."
- "Pause music."
- "What's playing right now?"

Audio Widgets and Complications

- Add a **music tile** or **audio playback complication** to your watch face for instant access
- Customize layouts in the **Wearable app** or directly on the watch by long-pressing your watch face

Payments On-the-Go with Samsung Pay or Google Wallet

The Galaxy Watch 7 Series and Galaxy Watch Ultra make it easier than ever to make quick, secure payments right from your wrist. With **Samsung Pay** and **Google Wallet** built-in, you can leave your wallet at home and still pay for your morning coffee, groceries, or transit fare—all with a simple tap.

Setting Up Samsung Pay

Samsung Pay on the Galaxy Watch allows for **NFC-based tap-and-pay transactions** and works with many major banks and credit card providers worldwide.

To set up:

1. Open the **Samsung Wallet** app on your watch

2. Follow the on-screen prompts to **sign in to your Samsung account** (if not already signed in)

3. On your phone, open the **Samsung Wallet** or **Galaxy Wearable** app

4. Tap **Add Card**, then scan or enter your credit or debit card details

5. Follow your bank's verification process

6. Once verified, your card is saved to the watch and ready to use

You can add multiple cards and select a **default card** for quicker payments.

Making a Payment with Samsung Pay

1. Press and hold the **Back button** (lower side button)

2. The card screen will appear—swipe to select a different card if needed

3. Hold your watch near the payment terminal (usually the same place you'd tap a card or phone)

4. Wait for the terminal to beep or display a confirmation message

5. You're done—no need to open your wallet or phone

Using Google Wallet

Google Wallet offers a similar NFC tap-to-pay function, especially useful if you're already using it on your Android phone.

To set it up:

1. Open the **Google Wallet** app on your Galaxy Watch

2. Tap **Get Started** and follow the instructions

3. On your phone, open the **Google Wallet** app

4. Add a new card or sync your existing cards to the watch

5. Complete the verification process for each card

6. Set up a **screen lock** on your watch—required for security before enabling payments

Making a Payment with Google Wallet

1. Double-press the **Home button** (top side button by default)

2. Your default card will appear

3. Hold the watch near the payment reader until the transaction is complete

4. You'll receive a confirmation vibration or sound

Payment Safety and Security

- Both Samsung Pay and Google Wallet use **tokenization**, meaning your actual card number is never shared with the terminal

- Payments require your watch to be **unlocked** and securely strapped to your wrist

- If the watch is removed, you'll need to **re-enter your PIN or pattern** before you can pay again

- You can manage, suspend, or remove payment cards remotely using your Samsung or Google account if your watch is lost

Tips for Smooth Payments

- Look for **contactless payment symbols** at the checkout terminal

- Keep **NFC enabled** (Settings > Connections > NFC)

- Wear your watch on your **dominant hand** for easier positioning at payment terminals
- Use **quick shortcuts** or gestures (like double-pressing a button) to launch your wallet faster

Chapter 7

Communicating and Staying Social

Sending and Receiving Texts

Your Galaxy Watch offers multiple ways to send and respond to text messages, all optimized for convenience and speed.

Supported Messaging Platforms:

- **Samsung Messages**
- **Google Messages**
- **WhatsApp**
- **Telegram** (via third-party app or notifications)
- Any other messaging app with notification support on your phone

How to Send a Message:

1. Tap the **Messages** app.
2. Select a contact or start a new message.
3. Choose your input method:
    - **Voice-to-text** (fastest and most natural)
    - **Keyboard** (QWERTY or T9 layout)
    - **Handwriting input** (draw letters on the screen)
    - **Quick replies** (custom or default messages like "On my way" or "Call you later")

Replying to Messages from Notifications:

When a message comes in:

- Tap the notification to expand it.

- Swipe up to reveal quick replies or choose "Reply."

- Use voice, text, or emoji to respond.

- If you miss a message, you can view and respond from the **Messages** app.

Customizing Quick Replies:

1. Open the **Galaxy Wearable** app on your phone.
2. Tap **Notifications > Quick Replies**.
3. Add or edit your preferred one-tap responses.

Voice Typing for Hands-Free Messaging

The built-in microphone makes voice typing fast and convenient:

- Activate any text field and tap the **microphone icon**.

- Speak your message clearly and wait for transcription.

- Tap **Send** to deliver your message.

- Works best in quiet environments or with earbuds for improved accuracy.

Contact Management on the Watch

Your watch syncs your phone's contact list automatically, so you can access, call, or message anyone from your wrist.

Viewing Contacts:

- Open the **Contacts** app on your watch

- Scroll through or use the **search bar** to find names

- Tap a contact to view call, message, or email options

Adding Favorites:

1. Open a contact on your watch
2. Tap **Add to Favorites**
3. Favorite contacts appear at the top of your list or as tiles for faster access

Sync Settings:

- Manage which contact accounts sync to your watch in the **Galaxy Wearable app** under **Watch Settings > Accounts and Backup > Sync Contacts**
- You can choose to sync from Google, Samsung, or other connected accounts

Connecting Social Media and Messaging Apps

Your Galaxy Watch 7 Series and Galaxy Watch Ultra aren't just great for calls and texts—they also keep you engaged with your favorite social platforms and messaging services. Whether you're staying in touch via WhatsApp, checking Instagram updates, or catching up on group chats through Telegram, your watch offers streamlined access to what matters, all without reaching for your phone.

How Social Media Integration Works

While most full social media apps (like Instagram, Facebook, or TikTok) aren't available natively on the watch due to screen and performance limitations, the Galaxy Watch connects with them in other smart ways:

- **Notification Mirroring**: Your watch displays notifications from social apps installed on your phone. You can read messages, view comments, see who liked a post, and respond where supported.

- **Quick Reply Support**: For messaging-based apps like WhatsApp, Telegram, and Facebook Messenger, you can reply directly from the watch using text, voice-to-text, emojis, or predefined quick responses.

- **Voice Commands**: Use Bixby or Google Assistant to send messages or open apps when supported. For example, "Send a WhatsApp message to Clara."

- **Smart Notifications Management**: Customize how and when social alerts reach your wrist.

How to Enable Notifications from Social Media Apps

1. On your phone, open the **Galaxy Wearable** app.
2. Tap **Watch settings > Notifications**.
3. Scroll through your list of installed apps.
4. Turn on notifications for apps like **Instagram**, **Facebook**, **Twitter**, **Messenger**, **WhatsApp**, **Telegram**, or **Snapchat**.
5. If needed, adjust settings in each app on your phone to allow lock screen or push notifications—these must be enabled for the watch to receive them.

Once enabled, your watch will vibrate or light up when you get a message, mention, or direct alert. You can tap the notification to expand and see full content or take action.

Viewing and Interacting with Notifications

- Tap once to open the full notification.
- Swipe up to see the full message or comment.
- Choose a quick reply or tap "Reply" to type or dictate a message.
- Some apps (like Instagram or Facebook) may only allow you to view the notification without reply options.

Apps That Work Well with Notification Replies:

- **WhatsApp** – Supports replies, voice messages (via mic), emojis
- **Telegram** – Supports replies and text input
- **Facebook Messenger** – Supports reply options depending on your phone
- **Signal and Viber** – Basic message viewing and reply support
- **Instagram DMs, Twitter, Snapchat** – Read-only notifications

Using WhatsApp and Telegram from Your Watch

These two apps offer some of the best messaging experiences on your Galaxy Watch, especially when you're busy or on the move. While there are no standalone full-featured apps for them on the watch (yet), the Galaxy Watch 7 Series and Ultra offer **deep notification-based interactions** and limited **third-party companion apps** for Telegram.

WhatsApp on Galaxy Watch

What You Can Do:

- **Read messages**: View incoming WhatsApp messages and group chats directly on your watch.
- **Reply instantly**: Use voice-to-text, the on-screen keyboard, or quick replies like "Yes," "No," "On my way," or custom responses.
- **Send emojis**: Tap the emoji icon to select from your favorites.
- **Mute or manage chats**: Long-press a notification to mute future alerts or block them temporarily.
- **View media**: While images and videos don't display on the watch screen, you'll be notified they were sent.

How to Enable WhatsApp Notifications:

1. Open **Galaxy Wearable > Notifications**
2. Ensure **WhatsApp** is toggled on
3. On your phone, go to **Settings > Notifications > WhatsApp** and allow full notification access
4. Enable **Message Previews** and **Notification categories** (especially for messages and group alerts)

Voice Replies on WhatsApp:

- Tap the microphone icon
- Speak naturally
- The watch converts your speech to text and sends it immediately

This is incredibly useful during workouts, meetings, or while driving—no need to type or touch your phone.

Telegram on Galaxy Watch

Telegram offers a slightly more advanced experience due to its open API and better Wear OS support. While there is **no official Telegram Wear OS app**, some third-party options like **"Pulse for Telegram"** or **"Weargram"** can enhance functionality.

What You Can Do with Notifications:

- **Read entire message threads** (text only)
- **Reply using voice or text**
- **React with emojis or thumbs-up responses**

- **Receive message previews with sender name and group info**

Using Third-Party Telegram Apps (Optional):

Apps like **Weargram** (available on the Play Store) can provide basic Telegram message browsing and replies:

1. Download the app on both your phone and your Galaxy Watch
2. Log in using your Telegram account (via QR or phone verification)
3. Access recent messages, reply, and browse contacts directly on your watch
4. Notifications remain in sync with your phone

Security and Privacy Considerations:

- WhatsApp and Telegram use end-to-end encryption, but your watch's **notifications are visible if your screen is unlocked.**

- Set a **PIN or pattern lock** for extra protection under **Settings > Security > Lock Type**

- Consider turning off **notification previews** for these apps if you want more discretion on your wrist

Tips for Efficient Messaging from Your Watch:

- Use **voice replies** whenever possible—it's the fastest input method
- **Customize your quick replies** with phrases you use often
- Turn on **Do Not Disturb** during focused work sessions to limit distractions
- Use **Message History** (in the Messages app) to revisit recent replies and threads

- Pair with **Bluetooth earbuds** for discreet voice messages during calls or noisy environments

Sharing Location and Staying Safe with Emergency Features

Your Galaxy Watch 7 Series and Galaxy Watch Ultra are more than fitness and communication tools—they're safety companions designed to support you in real-life emergency scenarios. Whether you're hiking alone, running at night, cycling on open roads, or simply living independently, these devices can share your real-time location, trigger safety alerts, and contact help when needed.

Setting Up Emergency Contacts and Location Sharing

Before you can use any safety feature, you'll need to assign emergency contacts and allow your watch to access location data.

How to Set Up Emergency Contacts:

1. Open **Settings** on your Galaxy Watch
2. Scroll to and tap **Safety and Emergency**
3. Select **Emergency Contacts**
4. Tap **Add Contact**, then choose from your synced phone contacts
5. Add up to **three emergency contacts**
6. Enable **location sharing and SOS messages**

Enabling Location Access:

1. On the watch, go to **Settings > Connections > Location**
2. Turn on **Location**
3. For more accuracy, enable **Wi-Fi and GPS** when available

4. Ensure location services are also enabled on your paired phone

Once this is set up, your Galaxy Watch can send your real-time location through SMS or Samsung Messages during emergencies.

Using SOS: Triggering Emergency Alerts

The Galaxy Watch allows you to discreetly alert your emergency contacts and send them your location, even if you can't speak or unlock your phone.

How SOS Works:

- Press the **Home button (top side key) three times quickly**
- The watch will vibrate, display a countdown (which you can cancel), and then:
  - Send an **emergency alert** with your **real-time GPS location**
  - Send a **pre-written message** like "I need help" or your custom text
  - Optionally include a **5-second audio recording** from your surroundings
  - Attempt to **call emergency services** if enabled and supported in your region

To Set Up SOS:

1. Go to **Settings > Safety and Emergency > Send SOS**
2. Turn on **SOS with Home Key**
3. Add or confirm **emergency contacts**
4. Customize the **emergency message** (e.g., "This is John. I need help. My location is attached.")
5. Choose to **include a voice recording** for extra context

6. Enable **auto call to emergency services** (optional; requires LTE or Bluetooth connection to phone)

Customizing SOS Settings:

- You can **enable a countdown** before the SOS is sent to prevent false alarms
- You can choose to share **location updates every 15 minutes** for a set duration
- For countries with eCall services, you can enable **direct emergency dialing**

Live Location Sharing for Real-Time Tracking

The **Live Location Sharing** feature allows your trusted contacts to track your location during an ongoing emergency or activity.

To Enable Live Location Sharing:

1. Open **Settings > Safety and Emergency > Share Location**
2. Add emergency contacts if not already done
3. Turn on **Allow location sharing**
4. During an emergency (SOS or fall detection), your watch will:
   - Send your GPS coordinates
   - Share a **real-time location link** (clickable in SMS)
   - Optionally record ambient audio

This feature is ideal for solo travelers, joggers, cyclists, and anyone in remote areas. Even if your phone battery dies, **LTE models** can share your location independently.

Fall Detection and Safety Alerts Explained

What Is Fall Detection?

Fall Detection is a built-in safety feature that uses your watch's sensors to recognize a hard fall followed by a lack of movement. If it detects that you've fallen and you don't respond within a short time frame, it triggers an automatic SOS alert to your emergency contacts—potentially life-saving in serious incidents.

How It Works:

1. The watch detects **a sudden change in acceleration** followed by **stillness or irregular movement**
2. It vibrates and displays a screen asking:
   - "Did you fall?"
   - With options: **I'm OK**, **Emergency Call**, or **Dismiss**
3. If no response is given within **60 seconds**:
   - It sends an **SOS alert** to your emergency contacts
   - Shares your **current location** and optional **audio recording**
   - Calls **emergency services** (if you have LTE or phone pairing)

How to Turn On Fall Detection:

1. On your Galaxy Watch, go to **Settings > Safety and Emergency > Hard Fall Detection**
2. Toggle it ON
3. Choose when to monitor for falls:
   - **Always**
   - **During physical activity only**
4. Ensure emergency contacts and SOS features are properly configured

5. Optionally enable automatic emergency calling if supported by your region and carrier

Fall Detection Accuracy and Limitations

The Galaxy Watch's accelerometer and gyroscope are finely tuned, but not every fall may be detected. Here's how to optimize its reliability:

Works Best When:

- The watch is **snug and properly worn on the wrist**
- You're engaging in **dynamic activities** (walking, jogging, biking)
- LTE or phone connectivity is active for calls and SMS

Might Not Detect Falls If:

- You fall **slowly** or onto a soft surface

  You **catch yourself** mid-fall
- You're engaging in **contact sports** or abrupt movements unrelated to falling

False alarms may occasionally occur during **high-impact workouts or jumps**, but these can be dismissed easily.

Emergency Call Features (LTE or Paired Phone)

If your watch has LTE:

- It can **call emergency services directly** without needing your phone
- You can **speak through the built-in mic and speaker**
- Call history will reflect the emergency dial for recordkeeping

If you're using Bluetooth only:

- The watch **relays the SOS through your connected phone**
- Your phone must be within range and unlocked (if necessary)

Medical Information Display

In case of an emergency, first responders can access your essential medical info even if the watch is locked.

To enable:

1. Go to **Settings > Safety and Emergency > Medical Info**
2. Input your:
   - Name
   - Date of birth
   - Blood type
   - Allergies
   - Existing medical conditions
   - Emergency contact numbers
3. This info is displayed when **"Emergency"** is tapped on the lock screen or alert prompt

Extra Safety Tips:

- Keep your **watch battery above 20%** when out alone
- Enable **Auto Brightness and Wake Gestures** so alerts are clearly visible
- Wear the watch on your **dominant wrist** for better sensor accuracy
- Practice triggering SOS in a safe environment so you understand the response flow

- Regularly update your emergency contact info and message in the **Galaxy Wearable app**

Chapter 8

Mastering Battery Life and Charging

Understanding Your Watch's Battery Life

Each model has a different battery size tailored to its features:

- The **Galaxy Watch 7 (40mm)** comes with a 300mAh battery
- The **Galaxy Watch 7 (44mm)** steps up to 425mAh
- The powerhouse **Galaxy Watch Ultra** packs a robust 590mAh battery

On a typical day, you can expect:

- Up to **2 days** of battery life on the standard Galaxy Watch 7
- And up to **2.5 days**, or even more, with the Galaxy Watch Ultra—especially if you manage your settings wisely

Here's what affects how long your battery lasts:

Your Screen Brightness and Display Settings:

The brighter your screen and the longer it stays on, the faster your battery drains. If you use the **Always-On Display**, that sleek look costs a bit more power throughout the day.

Health Tracking Running in the Background:

Keeping tabs on your heart rate, oxygen levels, stress, sleep, or all of the above? It's incredibly helpful—but those sensors are working behind the scenes around the clock, using battery life to give you insights.

Outdoor Activities with GPS:

Love tracking your hikes, runs, or bike rides? The GPS is one of the most power-hungry features, especially if set to high-accuracy mode. If you're going on a long adventure, it's smart to check your battery before you head out.

LTE and Wi-Fi Use:

If your watch is an LTE model and you're streaming music, taking calls, or sending messages without your phone nearby, it's convenient—but your battery will drain faster than when connected to your phone via Bluetooth.

Notifications, Apps, and Even Your Watch Face:

Lots of notifications, apps refreshing in the background, and even flashy or animated watch faces all add to your power usage. Choosing a simpler face and trimming unnecessary alerts can help your watch last longer.

Checking Your Battery Status

Want to know where your battery's going? Just go to **Settings > Battery** on your watch. You'll see what percentage is left and a breakdown of what's using the most energy—like health tracking, apps, or display time.

If something looks off—like a particular app using way more than the rest—it might be worth restarting your watch or removing that app to see if it improves.

What to Expect Day to Day

Keep in mind: the more you ask your watch to do, the faster the battery will go. Some days, when you're using GPS, playing music, answering calls, or checking messages frequently, it might drain quicker than on days when you're just tracking steps and checking the time.

After a software update, you might notice battery life dips slightly for a day or two—that's normal. Your watch is working behind the scenes to update, reindex, and optimize.

Smart Alerts and Built-In Efficiency

Your watch is smart enough to help you out with battery life. It will give you a heads-up when it drops below **15%**, and it can suggest switching to **Power Saving Mode** if it thinks you'll need more time. You'll also get alerts if apps are running too much in the background or if your location services have been on for a while.

Simple Ways to Charge Your Watch

Charging your Galaxy Watch 7 Series or Galaxy Watch Ultra is designed to be seamless and wireless, so you can spend less time worrying about battery levels and more time enjoying what your watch offers. There are several reliable ways to recharge your device, whether you're at home, in the office, or outdoors.

1. Use the Official Wireless Charging Dock (Magnetic Puck)
Your watch includes a dedicated **Samsung wireless charging puck** that uses **USB-C** for power. It's compact, magnetic, and travel-friendly.

To charge:

- Place the **back of the watch flat** onto the magnetic charging pad
- The charger will **align automatically** and hold the watch in place
- A charging animation or battery icon appears on the screen, showing that the device is charging
- Leave the watch on the charger undisturbed for optimal efficiency

This method is the most reliable and recommended by Samsung for maintaining battery health.

2. Fast Wireless Charging (Select Models Only)

The **Galaxy Watch 7 (44mm)** and **Galaxy Watch Ultra** support **fast wireless charging**, which significantly reduces downtime:

- **30 minutes** can deliver up to **45–50% battery**, ideal for quick recharges between meetings, workouts, or meals
- A full charge typically completes in **around 80–90 minutes**, depending on the model and current battery state

To access fast charging:

- Use a **15W or higher Samsung-approved charging adapter**
- Plug the charger directly into a **wall outlet** for best results (avoid USB hubs or low-output laptop ports)
- Avoid using the charger in **hot environments**, as thermal throttling can slow charging speed

3. Charging On-the-Go with a Power Bank

When you're away from a wall outlet, a **portable power bank** with USB-C output can charge your watch using the wireless puck:

- Connect the charging puck to the power bank via USB-C
- Lay the watch on the puck as you would normally
- Use a **power bank with a stable output** (at least 5V/2A) to ensure uninterrupted charging
- Keep the puck and watch in a flat, secure spot to avoid disconnection

Some power banks also offer **wireless charging pads**—though not all are compatible with the Galaxy Watch, so check product specs first.

4. Tips for Charging Safely and Effectively

- **Keep it dry:** Never charge your watch if it's wet. Rinse off sweat, chlorine, or saltwater, then dry thoroughly with a soft cloth

- **Remove metal accessories:** Don't place coins, keys, or metallic bands near the charging pad—they can interfere with the magnetic connection and cause overheating

- **Use only approved chargers:** Third-party chargers may cause battery degradation or heating issues over time. Stick to Samsung or certified accessories

- **Avoid overnight overheating:** If you charge overnight, place the charger in a well-ventilated space to prevent heat buildup

- **Store your charger safely:** The magnetic puck is small and can be misplaced easily—consider keeping a spare at work or in your travel bag

Tips to Get the Most from Every Charge

Even with powerful batteries and efficient chips, battery life can vary depending on how you use your watch. The good news is, with a few smart adjustments, you can significantly extend your battery between charges—whether you're at work, out on a hike, or managing a packed schedule.

1. Control Connectivity Features

- **Turn off Wi-Fi** when you're not using it—your phone connection via Bluetooth is usually sufficient for syncing

- If you're not using your earbuds or accessories, **disable Bluetooth** to conserve power

- When you're in low-signal areas or traveling, use **Airplane Mode** to stop your watch from constantly searching for networks

- On LTE models, disable **Mobile Data** unless needed, as cellular activity drains battery faster than Bluetooth or Wi-Fi

2. Adjust Display Settings

- **Lower your screen brightness** manually or enable **auto-brightness**
- Reduce **screen timeout** to 15 or 30 seconds
- **Turn off Always-On Display** unless you absolutely need it—it continuously consumes energy by keeping the screen active
- Choose a **simpler watch face** with fewer animations, background updates, or data-heavy widgets

3. Optimize Health and Wellness Tracking

While comprehensive health tracking is one of the watch's strengths, you can fine-tune it to balance performance and battery life:

- Change **heart rate monitoring** from "continuous" to "every 10 minutes" or "manual"

- Disable **SpO$_2$ monitoring** during sleep unless medically necessary
- Pause or reduce **stress tracking**, **snore detection**, and **skin temperature tracking** if they aren't a top priority
- Turn off **automatic workout detection** if you prefer starting workouts manually

4. Use Power Saving Features

The Galaxy Watch includes several smart power-saving tools built-in:

- **Power Saving Mode:** Temporarily limits background features like always-on connectivity, display animations, and app refreshes
  - Go to **Settings > Battery > Power Saving Mode**
  - Use it during travel, overnight, or low-battery situations

- **Watch-Only Mode:** Converts your smartwatch into a traditional timepiece, extending battery life to days—perfect for emergencies or minimal use
  - Activate via **Settings > Battery > Watch-Only Mode**

5. Limit Background Apps and Notifications

- Review which apps are allowed to run in the background by going to **Settings > Apps > App List**
- Close unused apps or uninstall those you don't use
- Limit **notification overload**—you don't need alerts from every app
  - Use the **Galaxy Wearable app > Notifications** to choose which apps can send alerts
  - Turn off notifications for social media, games, or promotions

6. Smart Charging Habits

- **Top off when needed**—even 10–15 minutes on the charger can give you several hours of use
- Avoid **fully draining** your battery often—it's better to recharge before it drops below 10%
- Unplug once fully charged to maintain long-term battery health
- If you charge overnight, consider using **slow charging pads** rather than fast chargers to reduce heat buildup

7. Use Battery Widgets and Alerts

- Add the **Battery widget** or tile to your watch screen for easy monitoring
- Keep an eye on your **estimated usage time** and take note of apps consuming power unusually fast
- Set low battery alerts if you often forget to charge before leaving for the day

1. Power Saving Mode

This mode helps conserve battery by turning off or limiting certain features while still allowing you to use your watch for essentials like time, notifications, steps, and heart rate tracking.

When enabled, Power Saving Mode will:

- Turn off Always-On Display
- Limit CPU speed and background activity
- Restrict app updates and background syncing
- Lower screen brightness
- Disable Wi-Fi, mobile data, and location (unless manually reactivated)
- Reduce screen timeout

How to activate:

- On your watch, go to **Settings > Battery > Power Saving Mode**, then tap **Turn On**
- Or swipe down on the main screen, tap the **Battery icon**, and select **Power Saving Mode**

You'll still receive important notifications and have access to key features, but with a significant improvement in battery duration.

2. Watch-Only Mode

This is your last-resort mode when the battery is very low, or you just want your device to function like a classic wristwatch for maximum endurance.

What it does:

- Disables all smart functions
- Displays only the time when you tap the screen or press a button
- Uses extremely low power

How to activate:

- Go to **Settings > Battery > Watch-Only Mode**
- You can also toggle this mode from the **Battery settings tile**

This mode can extend your battery for **days** if you're in a survival or travel situation where charging isn't possible.

3. Auto Battery Optimization Tips

Beyond power-saving modes, you can manually tweak settings for everyday efficiency:

- **Turn off tilt-to-wake** or adjust its sensitivity
- Switch heart rate monitoring to **interval-based** rather than continuous
- Reduce **notifications** to only essential apps
- Set your display to auto-brightness instead of max level
- Choose a **simple, low-power watch face** without animations or live updates

Battery Health Advice for Long-Term Use:

- **Avoid letting your watch drain completely** to 0% regularly—it's better to recharge around 10–20%
- **Unplug your watch** once it hits 100% to avoid keeping it at full charge for long periods
- **Don't charge your watch when it's hot** or after being in direct sunlight
- Stick to **Samsung-approved chargers** and avoid cheap third-party accessories
- If storing the watch unused for long periods, keep it at around **50% charge** and power it off

Wireless Power Sharing from Your Phone

One of the most convenient features available to Galaxy Watch users is **Wireless PowerShare**—Samsung's reverse wireless charging feature that lets you recharge your watch using the back of a compatible Galaxy smartphone.

What is Wireless PowerShare?

It allows your phone to act as a wireless charging pad for other devices—like your Galaxy Watch, Galaxy Buds, or another phone. It's perfect for quick top-ups when you're away from an outlet.

Compatible Phones Include:

- Galaxy S23/S24 Series
- Galaxy Z Fold and Flip Series
- Galaxy Note 20 and newer
- Select Galaxy A-Series models with wireless charging support

How to Use Wireless PowerShare:

1. Swipe down on your phone's home screen to access the **Quick Settings Panel**
2. Tap **Wireless PowerShare** (you may need to add the icon manually if it's not visible)
3. Place your Galaxy Watch **face up** on the center-back of the phone—align it carefully over the charging coil
4. A vibration and light will indicate that charging has started
5. Keep both devices still until the desired charge level is reached

Charging Speed and Considerations:

- Charging via PowerShare is **slower than standard charging**, so it's best for quick top-ups, not full recharges
- Works best when both devices are **not in use** and laid on a **flat surface**
- Remove bulky phone cases that might block the wireless charging connection
- Your phone must have **at least 30% battery** to begin Wireless PowerShare
- Turn off **your phone's screen and background apps** for faster charging efficiency

When to Use Wireless PowerShare:

- During travel when you forget your watch charger

- On long hikes or outdoor activities when your phone still has plenty of battery

- As a backup option in the office, airport, or car

- To charge your Galaxy Watch Ultra during short breaks between high-performance GPS tracking or workouts

Safety Tips:

- Avoid using PowerShare in **extremely hot environments**—charging generates some heat

- Don't attempt to charge if your watch is **wet or sweaty**—dry it thoroughly first

- Disconnect once charging is complete to avoid draining your phone unnecessarily

Chapter 9

Troubleshooting and Care Tips

Common Issues and Simple Fixes

Even though your Galaxy Watch 7 Series or Galaxy Watch Ultra is designed for performance and durability, every now and then, you might run into a small hiccup. Fortunately, most issues can be resolved with a few simple steps—no tech support needed. Here's a breakdown of common problems and how to solve them quickly, so you can get back to using your watch without frustration.

1. Watch Not Charging or Charging Slowly

Possible causes:

- Misalignment on the charging puck
- Dirty charging surface
- Using a non-Samsung or low-power charger
- Overheating

Fixes:

- Ensure the back of the watch is clean and dry
- Align it carefully on the charger until you feel it snap into place
- Use only Samsung-approved chargers or a power adapter that supports at least 15W
- Charge in a cool, well-ventilated area—if the watch feels warm, let it cool before trying again

2. Watch Not Turning On

Possible causes:

- Battery is completely drained
- Software glitch
- Hardware failure (rare)

Fixes:

- Connect the watch to the charger and let it sit for 10–15 minutes
- Press and hold both the **Home** and **Back buttons** together for 10 seconds to force a restart
- If it still doesn't turn on, try a different charging cable or adapter
- If there's no response after 30 minutes, contact Samsung Support

3. Watch Not Connecting to Phone

Possible causes:

- Bluetooth is off
- Watch or phone needs a restart
- Software update pending
- Galaxy Wearable app not syncing properly

Fixes:

- Make sure Bluetooth is turned on for both devices
- Restart both your phone and your watch
- Open the **Galaxy Wearable app**, check if it's requesting permissions or updates
- Try unpairing and re-pairing: go to **Bluetooth settings > Forget this device**, then reconnect

- Ensure both devices are on the latest software version

4. Notifications Not Showing Up

Possible causes:

- Notification permissions not granted
- Do Not Disturb or Sleep Mode is on
- Battery saver mode is limiting background activity

Fixes:

- On your phone, go to **Galaxy Wearable > Notifications**, and make sure your desired apps are toggled ON
- Check that your watch is not in **Theater Mode, DND, or Sleep Mode**
- Turn off **Power Saving Mode** if active
- Ensure the app itself (e.g., WhatsApp or Messages) is allowed to send notifications in your phone settings

5. Battery Draining Too Fast

Possible causes:

- Always-On Display is on
- GPS or LTE is running in the background
- Too many apps running or syncing constantly
- Continuous heart rate and sleep tracking

Fixes:

- Reduce screen brightness and timeout settings
- Turn off LTE, Wi-Fi, or GPS when not needed

- Disable Always-On Display

- Set heart rate monitoring to "Every 10 minutes" or "Manual"

- Check **Battery Usage** under Settings to see what's consuming power

6. Touchscreen Not Responding or Lagging

Possible causes:

- Software bug

- Water or sweat on the screen

- Background apps overloading memory

Fixes:

- Dry the screen completely if moisture is present

- Restart the watch

- Close unused apps

- If the problem continues, consider a **factory reset**:
  - **Settings > General > Reset** (back up your data first)

7. GPS Not Working Properly

Possible causes:

- Signal obstruction (dense buildings or trees)

- Low battery or Power Saving Mode enabled

- GPS settings misconfigured

Fixes:

- Make sure you're outdoors with a clear view of the sky

- Go to **Settings > Location**, and ensure GPS is turned ON

- Disable Power Saving Mode during workouts
- Wait a few minutes—GPS may take time to lock onto satellites in new areas

8. App Crashes or Freezing

Possible causes:

- App incompatibility
- Outdated software
- Storage full

Fixes:

- Update the app and your watch software
- Uninstall and reinstall the app from the Play Store
- Clear cached data or uninstall apps you no longer use
- Restart your watch to free up memory

9. Watch Getting Hot

Possible causes:

- Intensive tasks (GPS, LTE, workouts)
- Charging while in use
- Environment is too hot

Fixes:

- Pause usage and remove the watch until it cools
- Avoid using PowerShare and GPS-heavy apps at the same time
- Charge in a cool, dry place and don't charge immediately after intense activity

10. Software Update Issues

Possible causes:

- Watch or phone not connected to Wi-Fi
- Battery below 30%
- Interrupted downloads

Fixes:

- Ensure a strong Wi-Fi connection
- Make sure the battery is at least 50%
- Open the **Galaxy Wearable app > Watch Settings > Software Update**
- Restart the devices and try again

Restarting and Resetting Your Watch Safely

Just like any smart device, your Galaxy Watch 7 Series or Galaxy Watch Ultra may occasionally need a little help to get back on track. Maybe it's acting sluggish, an app freezes, or the connection to your phone seems off—don't worry, it happens. The good news is that most of these issues can be fixed with a simple restart. And if things still aren't running smoothly, a reset can give your watch a clean slate. Here's how to handle both—easily and safely.

Restarting: Your First Line of Defense

A restart is a quick way to refresh your watch without affecting your apps, data, or settings. Think of it like giving your watch a deep breath.

To restart your Galaxy Watch:

1. Press and hold the **Home (top right)** and **Back (bottom right)** buttons at the same time

2. Keep holding until the screen turns off and the **Samsung logo** appears

3. Release the buttons and let your watch reboot

This method is perfect when your watch freezes, becomes slow, or stops syncing properly with your phone.

When should you restart?

- Your apps won't open or are lagging
- Your watch stops syncing notifications
- Your display becomes unresponsive
- A software update just finished and things feel off

You can also restart by going to **Settings > General > Power > Restart** if your screen is still responsive.

Resetting: When You Need a Fresh Start

If restarting doesn't solve the issue—or you're planning to give your watch to someone else—a full reset may be the right move. Resetting wipes everything: your data, downloaded apps, settings, and synced accounts. It's like starting from scratch.

How to reset your watch safely:

1. On your watch, go to **Settings > General > Reset**
2. Tap **Reset**, then confirm when prompted
3. Your watch will power down, erase all data, and reboot like new

Before you reset, it's essential to **back up your data** so you can restore your settings and preferences later.

To back up your watch:

1. Open the **Galaxy Wearable** app on your phone
2. Tap **Watch settings > Accounts and backup > Back up data**
3. Select the data you want to save (like watch faces, health data, and apps)
4. Tap **Back up now**

This way, after the reset, you can sign in and restore your watch just the way you like it.

When is a reset the best choice?

- Your watch keeps disconnecting from your phone
- It's stuck in a loop or won't update
- You've installed a third-party app that's causing crashes
- You're selling or gifting the watch to someone else

It's also good practice to reset your watch before trading it in or returning it, so your personal information stays private.

Keeping Your Watch Updated and Secure

Your Galaxy Watch is a mini-computer on your wrist, and like your smartphone, it needs regular updates to stay fast, secure, and feature-rich. Software updates don't just bring new tools—they also fix bugs, improve battery life, and protect your data. Staying up to date is one of the easiest ways to get the best experience from your device.

How to check for updates:

On your watch:

1. Go to **Settings** > **Software update**
2. Tap **Download and install**
3. Follow the prompts if an update is available

Or from your phone (easiest method):

1. Open the **Galaxy Wearable** app
2. Tap **Watch settings** > **Watch software update**
3. Tap **Download and install**
4. If there's an update, your phone will send it directly to your watch

Make sure your watch is connected to Wi-Fi and has at least **50% battery** before starting the update.

Tips for smooth updating:

- Don't use the watch during the update—it needs uninterrupted time to install safely
- Keep it on the charger if the battery is low
- Restart the watch once the update completes to ensure all features initialize properly

Why updates matter:

- Fix glitches that might slow your watch down
- Improve health tracking accuracy
- Add new fitness modes, watch faces, or voice assistant features

- Patch security holes to protect your personal info

Protecting Your Watch: Smart and Simple Steps

Security isn't just about software—it's also about how you use your watch. Here's how to keep your data safe:

- **Set a screen lock:** Go to **Settings > Security > Lock type** and choose a PIN or pattern. This ensures no one can access your watch if it's off your wrist.

- **Enable auto-lock:** Set your watch to lock automatically when it's removed, so it stays secure even if lost.

- **Limit app permissions:** Review which apps have access to your location, microphone, contacts, or health data.

- **Stick to trusted apps:** Download apps from the **Google Play Store** only, and avoid unknown sources

- **Use SmartThings Find:** If your watch goes missing, use Samsung's **SmartThings Find** on your phone to locate, lock, or erase it remotely

- **Secure your Samsung and Google accounts:** Enable two-factor authentication so even if your watch is lost, your cloud data is safe

Caring for Your Galaxy Watch

watches get dirty. Whether it's sweat from a run, sunscreen at the beach, or dust during a hike, your watch deals with a lot. Taking a few seconds to clean it can prevent skin irritation, preserve its sensors, and keep it feeling fresh on your wrist.

- **Wipe it down daily** with a dry, soft cloth. After workouts or water exposure, give it a quick rinse with clean water and dry it thoroughly.
- If you've been in the ocean or pool, **rinse off salt or chlorine** to avoid corrosion over time.
- **Avoid using soaps, harsh chemicals, alcohol, or abrasive pads**—these can damage the finish and sensors.

Taking Care of the Band

The band not only keeps your watch secure—it also touches your skin all day. That means it needs some love, too.

- **Sport or silicone bands**: Rinse with water and mild soap, especially after sweating.

- **Leather bands**: Keep them dry. Wipe gently and avoid direct sunlight or moisture, which can cause cracking or discoloration.

- **Fabric bands**: Hand wash them occasionally and let them air dry.

If your band starts feeling itchy, sticky, or worn out, it's probably time to replace it. Thankfully, swapping out bands is super easy and a great way to change up your style.

Be Mindful of the Environment

Your watch is built to handle the elements, but it's still a smart device.

- Avoid **extreme heat or cold**. Leaving it on a hot car dashboard or exposing it to freezing temperatures for long periods can affect battery life and performance.

- If you're in a sauna, steam room, or hot tub—**take your watch off**. Prolonged exposure to heat and moisture can weaken seals over time.

- After swimming, **dry it off before charging**—never place a wet watch on the charger.

Charge Smart, Not Just Often

- Use the **official Samsung charger** or a certified equivalent.

- Don't charge overnight every single day—your battery prefers partial top-ups over full drains and long charging cycles.

- Charge on a flat surface away from metal objects. And always make sure your watch is dry first.

Keep It Running Smoothly

- Restart your watch every few days to clear up memory and refresh performance.

- Remove unused apps that may run in the background or drain battery.

- Regularly check for **software updates**—these often bring improvements that make your watch faster and more reliable.

- Back up your data using the **Galaxy Wearable app**, especially before a reset or a new phone pairing.

Contacting Samsung Support if You Need More Help

Even with all the right care, sometimes things just don't go as expected. Maybe your Galaxy Watch won't connect to your phone, a sensor stops working, or a weird bug pops up that doesn't go away. That's when it's time to call in backup—and Samsung has made it easy to get help when you need it.

Start with the Samsung Members App

If you have a Samsung phone, the **Samsung Members** app is already installed. It's your direct link to support, tips, and diagnostics.

- Open the app and tap **Get Help**
- Choose **Device care**, then select your Galaxy Watch
- You can run a quick **troubleshooting scan**, start a **live chat**, or book a **repair request** right from the app
- It also has user forums, FAQs, and step-by-step solutions for common problems

Visit the Samsung Support Website

Go to the Samsung website. Choose **Wearables > Galaxy Watch Series**, and you'll find:

- Easy-to-follow guides
- Warranty information
- Software update help
- Troubleshooting articles
- A link to **Live Chat** or **schedule a service appointment**

It's available 24/7, so you can get help whenever it's convenient.

Need Real-Time Support? Give Them a Call

If you prefer speaking to a real person, Samsung's customer care team is just a call away. You'll find the right number for your region on the website or inside the **Samsung Members** app.

Before you call, have this ready:

- Your watch's **model and serial number** (you'll find it under **Settings > About Watch**)
- A brief summary of what's going wrong
- The **troubleshooting steps** you've already tried
- Your **proof of purchase**, if you're asking about warranty support

In-Person Help: Samsung Service Centers

For hardware issues—like a cracked screen, unresponsive buttons, or water damage—you can visit a **Samsung-authorized service center** near you.

- Book an appointment online or walk in (depending on the location)

- Many centers offer **same-day repairs**

- You'll get an estimate before any work is done

- Repairs under warranty are usually free if there's no physical damage

Before handing over your watch, make sure to **back up your data** and **remove any personal straps** or accessories.

Bonus

Hidden Gems, Tips, and Tricks

Quick Shortcuts and Useful Gestures

Your Galaxy Watch 7 or Galaxy Watch Ultra is packed with features—but some of the most useful tools are easy to miss. Beyond the basics, there are hidden gems and time-saving tricks that can make your daily experience faster, smoother, and more personalized.

Master the Quick Panel (Your Command Center)

Swipe down from the top of the watch face to reveal the **Quick Panel**. This is your shortcut hub for toggling frequently used settings.

Here's what you can do:

- Tap **Wi-Fi, Bluetooth, or Airplane Mode** on or off instantly
- Adjust **brightness** without diving into Settings
- Enable **Do Not Disturb** during meetings or sleep
- Activate **Water Lock** before swimming to prevent accidental touches
- Use the **Flashlight** in dark spaces—your screen will turn bright white
- Tap **Battery Saver** when you're low on power
- Customize the layout by holding a tile and dragging it to a new spot

Double Press for Anything You Want

You can assign the **Home button's double press** to launch your favorite app or feature:

- Go to **Settings > Advanced features > Customize keys**

- Choose what a **double press** does: open an app (like Spotify or Timer), trigger a workout, or launch Bixby or Google Assistant
- You can also assign a **long press** to launch your preferred voice assistant

Raise Your Wrist, Wake Your Screen

This one's subtle but handy: your watch wakes up automatically when you raise your wrist. If it's not working smoothly:

- Go to **Settings > Display > Raise wrist to wake**, and make sure it's toggled ON
- Combine this with **Touch to wake** and **Tap screen to show time** for maximum responsiveness

Cover to Mute

If your watch rings during a meeting or moment of silence, just **place your palm over the screen**. It instantly silences alarms, calls, or timers—no buttons required.

Quickly Switch Between Apps

Want to multitask?

- **Double-press the Back button** to quickly return to your last-used app
- Swipe from the **edge of the screen** (on compatible models) to see recent apps
- Tap the icon to hop back in where you left off

Gesture Controls: Use Your Wrist to Control Your Watch

These clever gestures let you navigate without touching the screen.

To enable:

Settings > Advanced Features > Gestures

Available options:

- **Answer calls** by clenching and unclenching your fist twice
- **Dismiss alerts or decline calls** by rotating your wrist twice
- **Launch quick actions** like opening apps or toggling features with a customized wrist movement

It may feel funny at first—but once you get used to it, it's incredibly intuitive.

Pin a Favorite App or Tile

- Long-press on any **tile or app icon** to rearrange it
- Put your most-used apps (Messages, Workouts, Calendar) right up front
- Add custom tiles like a **water intake tracker**, **Spotify controls**, or a **daily steps goal**

Integrating Your Watch with Samsung Smart Home Devices

Your Galaxy Watch becomes even more powerful when it connects with your **Samsung SmartThings ecosystem**. From your wrist, you can control lights, adjust thermostats, check appliances, and more—all without reaching for your phone.

Get Started with SmartThings

1. Download and set up the **SmartThings** app on your smartphone
2. Add your smart devices (TVs, lights, plugs, fridges, AC units, etc.) to the app

3. On your Galaxy Watch, install the **SmartThings app** from the Play Store if it's not preinstalled

4. Log in with the same Samsung account you used on your phone

What You Can Do from Your Watch:

- **Turn off lights** or switch lighting scenes before bed
- **Adjust your thermostat** without leaving the couch
- **Start, pause, or check the status of your laundry**
- **Lock your smart door locks** or see if they're left open
- **Open your garage door** when you're biking back home
- **Control your Samsung Smart TV**—switch channels, change volume, pause Netflix
- **Trigger Routines**: for example, a "Good Morning" routine that turns on the lights, starts your coffee maker, and reads out the weather

Use Voice Control Too

- "Hey Bixby, turn off the living room lights."
- "Hey Google, is the front door locked?"
- Voice assistants on your watch can interact with SmartThings to control your home hands-free.

Create SmartThings Favorites

- Pin frequently used devices (like your bedroom lamp or TV) to the SmartThings widget on your watch for instant access
- Swipe to your tiles and control your home in seconds

Unlocking Hidden Features for Maximum Enjoyment

There's more beneath the surface of your Galaxy Watch—hidden gems that aren't always obvious but can dramatically enhance your experience once discovered.

1. Use Your Watch as a Camera Remote

Planning a group photo? Want to check your outfit before a meeting?

- Open the **Camera Controller app** on your watch
- It syncs with your phone's camera so you can preview the frame, switch lenses (if supported), and take pictures or videos remotely
- Perfect for selfies, tripod shots, or hands-free content creation

2. Navigate with Turn-by-Turn Directions on Your Wrist

If you use Google Maps or Samsung Maps, your watch can guide you turn by turn.

- Start navigation on your phone
- Your watch will automatically mirror the directions
- You'll get gentle haptic feedback and visual prompts for each turn

3. Sync Spotify and YouTube Music for Offline Playback

No phone? No problem.

- Open **Spotify or YouTube Music** on your watch
- Login and **download playlists or podcasts directly**
- Pair your watch with Bluetooth earbuds and hit the trail, gym, or commute—completely phone-free

4. Take Screenshots on Your Watch

- Press the **Home and Back buttons simultaneously**

- A quick flash will confirm the screenshot
- View it later in the **Gallery app**, or sync it to your phone automatically

5. Use Find My Phone (Or Watch!) Instantly

Lose your phone again?

- Open the **Find My Phone** tile
- Tap to make your phone ring—even if it's on silent
- If you misplace your watch, use **SmartThings Find** from your phone to make it vibrate or show its last known location

6. Track Your Water and Caffeine Intake

Stay on top of hydration and avoid that third coffee.

- Add the **Water intake and Caffeine** tiles
- Log your drinks with one tap
- Get reminders throughout the day to stay balanced

7. Share Your Live Location in Real-Time

For added safety or just letting someone know you're en route:

- Open **Safety and Emergency > Share Location**
- Add emergency contacts
- Trigger live location sharing with a **triple press of the Home button**

8. Use Modes & Routines for Automation

Create smart routines that change your settings based on time, activity, or location:

- Example: When it's bedtime, lower brightness, enable Do Not Disturb, and switch to a calming watch face
- When you arrive at the gym, launch the Workout app and enable Spotify

- These can run automatically—no swiping needed

Appendices

Technical Specifications Made Simple

Galaxy Watch 7 – 40mm & 44mm

Designed for everyday use, fitness tracking, and sleek style, the Galaxy Watch 7 is available in two sizes to suit different wrists and preferences—without compromising performance.

Sizes and Display:

- **40mm model**: Compact and lightweight, great for smaller wrists
  - Display: 1.3-inch Super AMOLED, Sapphire Crystal
  - Resolution: 432 x 432 pixels

- **44mm model**: Larger screen for easier visibility and more space for widgets
  - Display: 1.5-inch Super AMOLED, Sapphire Crystal
  - Resolution: 480 x 480 pixels

Both models feature **Always-On Display**, **auto-brightness adjustment**, and ultra-smooth touch responsiveness.

Build and Design:

- Armor Aluminum case
- Sapphire Crystal glass for scratch resistance
- Water resistance: **5ATM + IP68**, plus **MIL-STD-810H** durability certification
- Available in a range of finishes and interchangeable bands

Battery and Charging:

- **40mm**: 300mAh battery
- **44mm**: 425mAh battery
- Fast wireless charging (USB-C magnetic charger included)
- Typical usage: Up to 40 hours
- Power Saving Mode and Watch-Only Mode extend usage dramatically

Performance:

- Powered by Samsung's new **Exynos W1000 5-core processor**
- 2GB RAM + 32GB internal storage
- Runs on **Wear OS 4 with One UI Watch 5**
- Smooth app switching, voice assistant performance, and fitness tracking

Health and Sensors:

- **BioActive Sensor** (Heart Rate, SpO_2, and Bioelectrical Impedance Analysis)
- **Skin temperature sensor**
- **Accelerometer, barometer, gyro, geomagnetic sensor, light sensor**
- **Fall detection, irregular heart rate alerts, cycle tracking, sleep coaching**

Connectivity:

- Bluetooth 5.3
- Wi-Fi 802.11 a/b/g/n
- Optional LTE (on LTE models)
- NFC for contactless payments
- GPS/GLONASS/Galileo/BeiDou for location tracking

Compatibility:

- Android 10+ with at least 1.5GB RAM
- Not compatible with iOS

Galaxy Watch Ultra – 47mm

Built for explorers, athletes, and high-performance users, the Galaxy Watch Ultra is the rugged flagship in the family, blending precision, power, and premium features in a larger format.

Size and Display:

- 47mm case with enhanced durability
- 1.5-inch Super AMOLED display with higher peak brightness
- Sapphire Crystal glass with enhanced shatter resistance
- Resolution: 480 x 480 pixels
- Ultra-smooth visuals, Always-On Display, customizable brightness levels

Build and Durability:

- Titanium Grade 4 case (stronger than aluminum and lighter than steel)
- Sapphire Crystal glass
- Water resistance: **10ATM + IP68**, certified for **MIL-STD-810H** conditions
- Designed to endure extreme heat, cold, altitude, pressure, and moisture

Battery and Charging:

- 590mAh battery
- Fast wireless charging (USB-C charger)
- Up to **60 hours typical usage**, **100+ hours in Power Saving Mode**
- Optimized for long outdoor tracking and adventure use

Performance:

- Exynos W1000 processor
- 2GB RAM + 32GB storage
- Runs on Wear OS 4 with One UI Watch 5
- Handles multitasking, maps, workouts, voice commands, and streaming effortlessly

Advanced Sensors and Features:

- Dual-frequency GPS (L1 + L5) for ultra-precise location tracking
- BioActive Sensor with advanced **heart rate and body composition monitoring**
- Barometric altimeter, compass, and temperature sensor
- Specialized outdoor activity modes: **Trail Running**, **High-altitude Hiking**, **Multi-day Trekking**
- Emergency SOS and **track-back navigation** for remote safety
- Fall detection, route tracking, and location sharing in real-time

Connectivity:

- Bluetooth 5.3, Wi-Fi, LTE (on cellular models), NFC
- Compatible with SmartThings and SmartThings Find
- Samsung Pay / Google Wallet support
- Full voice assistant control with **Bixby** and **Google Assistant**
- Offline music and Spotify/YouTube Music downloads for phone-free adventures

Compatibility:

- Works with Android 10+ (1.5GB RAM minimum)
- Not compatible with iPhones

Compatible Smartphones and Operating Systems

Smartphones

To get the most from your Galaxy Watch, pair it with a smartphone that meets the following minimum requirements:

- **Operating System**: Android 10.0 or later
- **Memory**: At least 1.5GB of RAM
- **Bluetooth**: Version 5.0 or higher recommended
- **Samsung Wearable App Support**: Must be available in your region and compatible with your phone's app store (Google Play or Samsung Galaxy Store)

Fully Supported Android Devices Include:

- **Samsung Galaxy Phones**:
    - Galaxy S24/S23/S22/S21 Series
    - Galaxy Z Fold5, Z Flip5, Fold4, Flip4
    - Galaxy Note 20 and Note 10 Series
    - Galaxy A-Series (A54, A73, A34, A15, and others with Android 10+)

- **Other Major Android Phones:**
    - Google Pixel 5 and newer
    - OnePlus 9 and newer
    - Xiaomi, Oppo, Realme, Vivo, Motorola models running Android 10+

○ Sony Xperia devices with current Android software

Partially Compatible Devices (Limited Functionality)

Some Android phones may connect but offer **limited features**, especially if they don't support Samsung services or use heavily customized Android skins.

- Examples: older Huawei models (pre-Google ban), Nokia Android Go phones, Amazon Fire devices
- *Limitations may include:*
    - ○ No Samsung Health syncing
    - ○ No Galaxy Store or Samsung Pay
    - ○ Restricted access to Watch settings via Galaxy Wearable app

Your Samsung Warranty Explained Clearly

Your Galaxy Watch 7 Series or Galaxy Watch Ultra includes a limited manufacturer's warranty that protects against issues related to defects in materials or craftsmanship. Understanding the coverage helps ensure you know your options if anything goes wrong.

What's Covered:

- Defects caused by faulty materials or workmanship
- Battery issues not caused by user damage or aging
- Software malfunctions that interfere with the basic function of the watch
- Screen/display issues not caused by drops or cracks

What's Not Covered:

- Physical damage caused by accidents, misuse, or impacts
- Water damage resulting from use beyond rated depth or incorrect charging while wet
- Problems due to third-party accessories, chargers, or unauthorized repairs
- Cosmetic wear (scratches, discoloration)
- Theft, loss, or intentional damage
- Repairs by non-certified technicians or unofficial service providers

Warranty Period:

- Typically **1 year** from the date of purchase for the watch and included accessories
- Duration may vary by region—always check your proof of purchase for your local warranty terms

What You'll Need for Warranty Service:

- **Proof of purchase or receipt** showing the original date of sale
- Your device's **serial number** (found under **Settings > About Watch**)
- A brief description of the issue
- Your contact information

How to Get Warranty Support:

- Use the **Samsung Members app** on your phone to access customer support and run diagnostics
- You can call Samsung's customer service line to report issues and request guidance
- Warranty service may include repairs, replacements, or troubleshooting based on the issue

Easy-to-Understand Definitions of Common Terms

Active Zone Minutes

A measure of the time you spend in your target heart rate zones during exercise. It reflects how much meaningful activity you've done rather than just steps taken.

Always-On Display (AOD)

A feature that keeps your watch screen dimly lit at all times, showing the time and basic info without needing to tap or raise your wrist.

App Tile

A mini screen that shows live data from an app (like weather, calendar, or heart rate) and can be swiped through directly from your home screen.

Barometric Altimeter

A sensor that measures atmospheric pressure to estimate altitude. Useful for hiking, climbing, and elevation tracking.

Bixby

Samsung's built-in voice assistant that helps you control your watch using voice commands—like sending texts, starting workouts, or setting reminders.

Bluetooth

A wireless connection that allows your watch to sync with your phone, headphones, or other devices for data transfer and communication.

Body Composition

A feature that uses sensors to estimate body fat percentage, skeletal muscle mass, and body water levels, giving you a more complete picture of your health.

Complication

A small widget displayed on your watch face that shows live data like steps, battery level, or weather—customizable based on what matters to you.

Customization Keys

Settings that let you assign actions to button presses—such as launching an app when you double-press or long-press a button.

Cycle Tracking

A feature designed for women's health that helps monitor and predict menstrual cycles, ovulation, and related symptoms.

Do Not Disturb (DND)

A mode that silences all notifications, calls, and alerts for a set period—perfect for sleep, meetings, or focused time.

Fall Detection

A safety feature that senses if you've taken a hard fall and, if you don't respond, sends an SOS message to your emergency contacts.

Galaxy Wearable App

The companion app on your smartphone used to pair, customize, and manage your Galaxy Watch settings, watch faces, and notifications.

Gesture Controls

Motion-based shortcuts that let you answer calls, dismiss alerts, or trigger actions with wrist movements—no screen tap needed.

GPS

Global Positioning System—used for tracking your location, pace, and routes during outdoor activities like running, hiking, or biking.

Heart Rate Monitor

Built-in sensor that tracks your heartbeats per minute throughout the day and during workouts to assess intensity and recovery.

LTE (Cellular Connectivity)

Models with LTE allow you to use your watch for calls, messages, and data—even when your phone isn't nearby. Requires activation through your mobile carrier.

One UI Watch

Samsung's user interface for Wear OS, designed to make navigating your Galaxy Watch simple and familiar.

Power Saving Mode

A battery-saving setting that limits background activity, lowers brightness, and disables non-essential features to extend battery life.

Quick Panel

The control center you access by swiping down from the top of the screen—useful for toggling settings like Wi-Fi, brightness, and airplane mode.

Samsung Health

Samsung's health and fitness app that tracks activity, sleep, stress, heart rate, and more—available both on your watch and phone.

SmartThings

Samsung's smart home platform that lets you control lights, TVs, thermostats, and other connected devices from your Galaxy Watch.

SpO$_2$ (Blood Oxygen Saturation)

A measurement of how much oxygen is in your blood. This feature helps monitor respiratory health, especially during sleep or workouts.

Touch Bezel

A circular gesture control around the edge of the watch face that lets you scroll through menus, tiles, and apps with a simple swipe.

VO$_2$ Max

An advanced fitness metric estimating the maximum amount of oxygen your body can use during intense exercise. Helps assess your cardiovascular fitness.

Watch Face

The main screen of your watch. You can customize it with different styles, colors, and data widgets to match your taste and needs.

Wear OS

The operating system created by Google and used by Samsung on the Galaxy Watch 7 Series and Ultra—allowing app downloads from the Google Play Store.

www.ingramcontent.com/pod-product-compliance
Lightning Source LLC
LaVergne TN
LVHW060122070326
832902LV00019B/3095

* 9 7 9 8 2 8 0 0 6 6 5 2 6 *